MW00339156

LUDWIG VAN BEETHOVEN

32

SONATAS FOR THE PIANOFORTE

EDITED BY

ARTUR SCHNABEL

VOLUME ONE

SIMON AND SCHUSTER · NEW YORK

PUBLISHED BY SIMON AND SCHUSTER
A DIVISION OF GULF & WESTERN CORPORATION
SIMON & SCHUSTER BUILDING
ROCKEFELLER CENTER, 1230 AVENUE OF THE AMERICAS
NEW YORK, N.Y. 10020

23 24 25 26 27 28 29 30

ISBN 0-671-07100-9
MANUFACTURED IN THE UNITED STATES OF AMERICA

TABLE OF CONTENTS

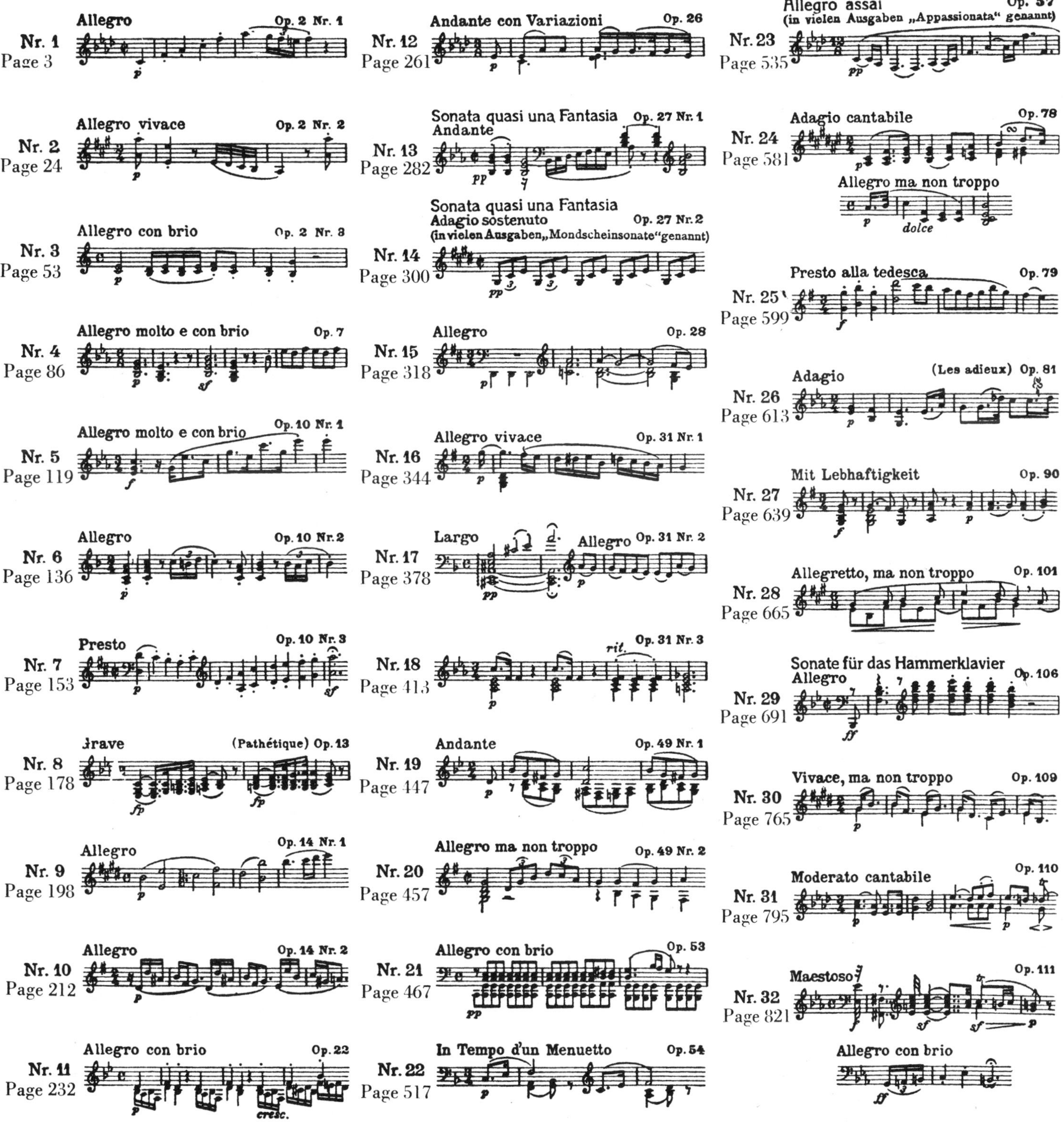

PUBLISHER'S PREFACE

(TO THE TENTH PRINTING)

ON August 15, 1951, Artur Schnabel died in Switzerland. He had had a profound influence on the musical life of the whole western world through his teaching, through his playing, through the devotion of hundreds of fine musicians inspired by his warm personality and profound musicianship.

Although Mr. Schnabel's own compositions were strictly in a twentieth century idiom, it was through his insight into classical music — particularly that of Mozart, Schubert, and Beethoven — that he made his most widely appreciated contribution to our musical heritage. His performances of these classics, whether heard in concert, on the air, or on discs, set a standard of scholarship, inspiration, and insight rarely equaled by any other pianist. They were the result of a lifetime of study of the great works — a study that never hardened into any single way of interpretation but always lived as though they had been planted in the solid ground of intellectual understanding and blossomed at the moment of performance in the air of a living, modern world.

In 1935, we were first entrusted by Mr. Schnabel with bringing out his edition of the Beethoven Sonatas. We counted it then, and still count it, as a signal honor. Today, with his discs, it remains the chief source of musical enlightenment from his great mind and heart. In preparing his edition, he went to the original manuscripts, when available, as well as to the original editions and to all subsequent editions. He respects, everywhere, the principle that the interpreter should play what the composer would have wanted to hear. And to carry this principle into editing practice, he has used all his vast knowledge of the history of style, his command of technique, and his mastery of pedagogy to supplement the scanty interpretative directions and fingerings afforded in the manuscripts and early editions.

The general principles are set forth in his very brief Preface, which, along with his notes, are given in this edition in three languages. Most of his notations are self-explanatory; but on account of the large number of queries we have received, we take this opportunity to point out that the Roman numerals, as well as the signs ╥, are an indication of the length of certain phrases which do not fit the conventional four-bar formula of most classical music. These, along with the thousands of other contributions made by Mr. Schnabel, should help the performer in achieving a new insight into the phrasing and the structure of the Sonatas.

THE PUBLISHERS

January, 1953

EDITOR'S PREFACE

THE fingering in this edition may here and there appear somewhat strange. In explanation of the more unusual kinds let it be said that the selection was not made exclusively with a view to technical facility, but rather from the desire to secure—at least approximately—the correct musical expression of the passages in question (as the Editor feels they should be interpreted). Quite often the Editor was guided by the pedagogic conception of a piano of which the tone colouring is unaided by the pedal—the fact being that the pedal is very seldom used in the classic piano literature as a means of colouring. In accordance with this conception the use of the pedal is rarely indicated in this edition. It must be the player's aim to succeed in rendering song-like passages, as if cast in *one* mould, without recurring to the pedal.

The fingerings and pedal indications are almost without exception by the Editor; the original texts, especially those of earlier works, contain next to none. The slurs as well as the accents and indications relative to touch were noted by the composer in such an obvious and confusing flightiness and carelessness—especially in his early works—that the Editor felt himself not only musically justified, but in duty bound to change them occasionally according to his best judgment, sense and taste: to abbreviate, to lengthen, to supplement, to interpret. Changes of this kind are not especially noted; all other additions made by the Editor are to be recognized either by smaller print or by brackets.

m. d. = right hand / m. s. = left hand.

ARTUR SCHNABEL

VORWORT

Manche Fingersätze dieser Ausgabe werden vielleicht befremden; zur Erklärung der ungewöhnlicheren sei gesagt, dass die Auswahl nicht ausschliesslich zur Bequemlichkeit der Hände getroffen wurde, dass sie vielmehr häufig dem Wunsche entstammt, den musikalischen Ausdruck der jeweiligen Stellen (wie ihn der Herausgeber meint) zu sichern oder mindestens nahezulegen. Dabei leitete ihn auch oft die erziehliche Vorstellung des Klavieres ohne klangliche Unterstützung durch das Pedal, das in der klassischen Klaviermusik sparsam und im Notfall, und nur sehr selten als Färbungsmittel verwendet wurde. Die Kargheit der Pedalisationshinweise entspricht dieser Auffassung; es ist zu erstreben (und zu erreichen), gesangartige Tonfolgen auch ohne Pedal-Leim wie aus einem Stück geformt erscheinen zu lassen.

Fingersätze und Pedalangaben sind fast ausnahmslos vom Herausgeber; die Originaltexte, zumal der früheren Werke, enthalten beinahe gar keine. Die Bindebogen (wie auch die Akzente und Anschlagarten) sind in den Vorlagen gelegentlich mit so offenkundiger, so verwirrender Flüchtigkeit und Sorglosigkeit aufgezeichnet,—hauptsächlich in den Frühwerken,—dass der Herausgeber das musikalische Recht, die musikalische Pflicht zu haben glaubte, sie mitunter nach Uberlegung, Sinn und Geschmack zu ändern: zu verkürzen, zu verlängern, zu ergänzen, zu deuten. Derartige Abweichungen sind nicht besonders kenntlich gemacht. Alle anderen Zusätze des Herausgebers aber sind ersichtlich aus kleiner oder eingeklammerter Schrift.

m. d. = rechte Hand / m. s. = linke Hand.

AVANT-PROPOS

Le doigté inusité que l'on trouvera par endroits dans cette édition surprendra peut-être. Si nous l'avons choisi, c'est moins pour la commodité des doigts que dans le but de fixer le caractère d'un passage — ou de le suggérer d'une façon approximative — selon les intentions de l'éditeur.

Souvent nous avons suivi l'idée—utile au point de vue pédagogique—d'un piano auquel manquerait l'appui de la pédale. Dans la musique classique, il est recommandable de ne faire usage de la pédale que modérément, en cas d'urgence; elle ne doit servir que rarement de «colorant». Aussi bien ne la trouvera-t-on prescrite qu'à fort peu d'endroits. Le pianiste devra s'efforcer de jouer les passages mélodiques «comme d'une pièce», sans avoir recours à la pédale. Il est possible d'y parvenir au prix de certains efforts.

Le doigté et les pédales sont presque exclusivement de la main de l'éditeur; les textes originaux en sont à peu près entièrement dépourvus; c'est là le cas en particulier des œuvres de jeunesse.

Dans ces textes, les arcs (de même que les accents et les indications relatives au jeu) ont été parfois notés très fugitivement et avec beaucoup de négligence, pouvant donner lieu à des erreurs; ici l'éditeur s'est cru le droit et même le devoir de transformer, de raccourcir, de rallonger, de compléter selon que le lui dictaient la raison, le sens du passage, le bon goût. Les transformations de ce genre ne sont pas mentionnées comme telles. Par contre toutes les autres adjonctions de l'éditeur sont imprimées en petits caractères ou placées entre crochets.

m. d. = main droite / m. s. = main gauche.

32

SONATAS FOR THE PIANOFORTE

LUDWIG VAN BEETHOVEN

SONATE

No. 1

JOSEPH HAYDN GEWIDMET

ALLEGRO (𝅗𝅥 = 126–138) *BEETHOVEN, Op. 2 Nr. 1*

con espressione
cresc.
p leggiero

a) Manche Ausgaben haben hier ein Auflösungszeichen; ich halte „des" für richtig.

a) Dans certaines éditions, nous trouvons ici un bécarre, je crois que „ré bémol" est juste.

a) In some editions a sign of resolution is to be found here; I consider "d♭" to be correct.

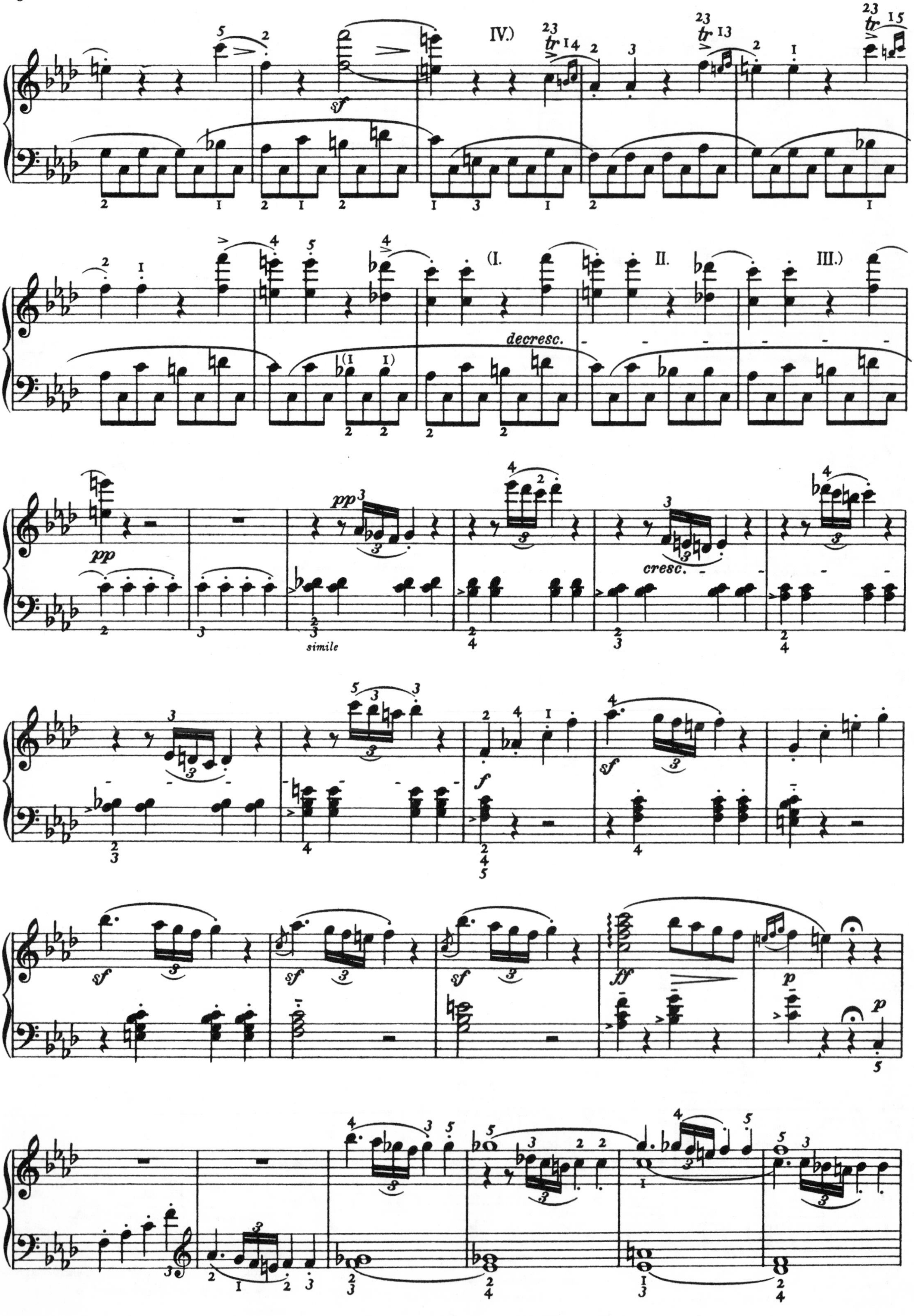
IV.)
tr
sf
(I.
II.
III.)
decresc.
pp
simile
cresc.
f
ff
p

(I. V.)

fp *p* *p*

sf *p* *sf*

cresc. *ff*

sf *sf* *pp* *ff* *sf* *sf* *sf*

p con espressione *sf* *cresc.* *sf* *f*

ff *ff* *sf* *sf* *sf* *ff*

ADAGIO (♪ = 88)
dolce
mp cantabile
molto p
pp
sf
rinf.
dim.
m.d.
(ruhig)
(calme)
(calm)

a)
b)
c)
poco dim.
dim.
mp cantabile
molto p

a)
(I.
II.
III.)
pp
sfp
tranquillo
poco
mp
b)
c)
mp cantabile
sempre legatissimo
Ped.
sempre dolce

dolce tranquillo
pp
poco più tranquillo
mp
p sonore
pp
sfp
p
sfp
p
sf
p
a)
b)
pp
pp
più pp
sf
a)
b)

MENUETTO

ALLEGRETTO (𝅗𝅥. = 58)

a) *Kurzer Vorschlag.*
Appogiature brève
Short appoggiatura.

b)

1) *ohne zu eilen* 1) *sans hâte* 1) *without haste*
2) *angenehm gefällig* 2) *plaisamment* 2) *pleasantly*

a) *Der untere Fingersatz ist von Beethoven.* | a) *Le doigté inférieur est de Beethoven.* | a) *The lower fingering has been prefixed by Beethoven.*

PRESTISSIMO (𝅗𝅥 = 116)
p leggiero, non troppo legato
IV. etc.
p dolce
a)
Ped.
a)
oder besser
ou mieux encore
or better still

a) Die Notierung der ersten Note jeder Triole als Viertel stammt vom Herausgeber.

a) C'est l'éditeur qui a donné à la première note de chaque triolet la valeur d'une noire.

a) The Editor has given the first note of every triplet the value of a crotchet.

dim.
più p
energico
f subito
ff subito
sempre ff
molto
mp
p
ff
(I.
II.
III.
I.
III.
IV.
V.)
Ped.

sempre piano e dolce, ma cantabile
pp
sempre simile
un
a)
poco più p
molto dolce
a)
mp
p
b)
più p
mf
a)
b)

un poco rubato
m. s.
dolce
non pressare
molto
a)

molto
Ped.
non troppo f
subito
senza Ped.
(I.
cresc.
II.
III.
I.
decresc.
IV.)

f
p
mp
mf
p
pp
p
pp
tr
tr
fp
mf
p
f
p
f
(I.
f
ff
sf
Ped.

1) melancholisch
mélancolique
in a melancholy vein

più p
poco
molto p
f
Ped.
ff
sfz

SONATE

No. 2

JOSEPH HAYDN GEWIDMET

BEETHOVEN, Op. 2 Nr. 2

a) *Ausführung mit einer Hand zwar schwerer, aber schwungvoller, als in beide Hände geteilt.*	a) *L'exécution de ce passage par une main seule est plus difficile main fait plus d'effet que si on distribue le passage aux deux mains.*	a) *The execution of this passage by one hand only is more difficult, but it sounds more sonorous than if divided between both hands.*

a) *In keiner Originalausgabe ist vermerkt, wann nach dem „rallentando" das erste Zeitmaß einzusetzen habe; nach meiner Ansicht soll es bei „dis d" eintreten.*

a) *Aucune édition originale n'indique où doit recommencer le tempo primo après le „rallentando." Je suis d'avis de le reprendre au „ré dièze d".*

a) *No mention is made in any of the original editions as to when the original tempo recurs after the „rallentando;" in my opinion, it should be at „d sharp d".*

a)

b)

c)

a)

b) Es ist, wie die diesbezügliche Verschiedenheit der Ausgaben erkennen läßt, unklar, ob hier, wie auch 2 Takte später als obere Wechselnote der Halb- oder der Ganzton zu nehmen sei; ich halte den Ganzton für den richtigen, also:

was im übrigen auch der Parallelstelle entspricht.

b) On ne sait pas – et les éditions diffèrent à ce sujet – s'il faut prendre ici et 2 mesures plus tard pour note appogiature supérieure le demi-ton ou un ton entier; j'estime qu'un ton entier est plus juste:

ce qui correspond d'ailleurs au passage parallèle.

b) The various editions differ as to whether here – as well as 2 bars later – the whole or the half tone is to be taken as the upper appoggiatura; in my opinion, the whole tone is correct, thus:

this also corresponds with te parallel passage.

c)

1) *nicht eilig, nicht überstürzt*
sans hâte ni précipitation
no hurry, no precipitation!

a) *Mit einer Hand sehr schwer auszuführen (es soll aber jedenfalls immer wieder versucht werden): die zweckdienlichste und übliche Spielweise:*

a) *Très difficile à jouer d'une main (il faudrait néanmoins faire et refaire l'expérience); voici la manière habituelle, qui est la plus conforme au but désiré.*

a) *Very hard of execution with one hand (it should always be tried however); the most efficient and customary way of playing this passage is this:* —

Auch bei der Aufwärtsbewegung das erste Triolen-Sechzehntel mit der Linken, zweites und drittes mit der Rechten zu nehmen, erscheint mir mühevoller (und weniger glänzend) als die vorstehende Einteilung.

Même répartition des mains en remontant. Il me semble qu'on a plus de peine et que l'on gagne moins d'effet à vouloir, en remontant, jouer la première double-croche du triolet de la main gauche, la 2e et la 3e de la main droite.

To take the first triole-semiquaver with the left hand, the second and third with the right hand also in the upward movement, appears to me to be more laborious (and less brilliant) than the preceding arrangement.

b) *Siehe a)*
voir a)
see a)

c) *Das h wird (selbsttätig) die hier nötige Kraft erhalten, wenn es von der rechten Hand genommen wird; das sfz gilt nur ihm, nicht auch dem dis.*

c) *En jouant le si de la droite, on lui donnera automatiquement la force que nécessite ce passage; le sfz se rapporte uniquement au si; il ne s'applique plus au ré dièze.*

c) *The „b" will obtain, automatically, the necessary strength if taken with the right hand; the sfz only refers to this „b", not to the „d sharp" also.*

d) *Ein hier in manchen Ausgaben hinzugefügtes e ist wohl falsch.*

d) *Dans un certain nombre d'éditions, un ré se trouve interpolé ici; il s'agit probablement d'une erreur.*

d) *A „d" is here interpolated in some editions, which is obviously erroneous.*

a) Zweifellos g, nicht es, wie einige Ausgaben glaubten, verbessern zu müssen.

1) wuchtig / pesamment / weighty

a) Il n'y a pas de doute qu'il faille sol, et non pas mi bémol; comme certaines éditions out cru devoir le corriger.

a) Undoubtedly „g," and not „e flat," as erroneously „corrected" in some editions.

m. s.
meno ff
ff
Ped.
m. s.
meno ff
sffz
Ped.
m. s.
meno ff
sffz
Ped.
Ped.
ff
ff
p
pp
p subito
pp
Ped.
fp
pp
p
pp
pp
p
p
pp
pp
leggiero
p
fp
fp
pp
dolce
p
pp
fp

a) *Manche Ausgaben haben hier (gleichlautend mit dem viertnächsten Takt) gis, a, h, gis in der obersten Stimme; reizvoller ist gewiß, die beiden Takte verschieden zu lassen.*	**a)** *Certaines éditions ont à cet endroit: sol ♯, la, si, sol♯ dans la voix supérieure, tout comme le passage qui vient 4 mesures plus tard; l'effet est certainement plus agreable, si l'on laisse subsister la différence.*	**a)** ***Some editions have here (the same as in the 4th following bar) g sharp, a, b, g sharp in the upper part; it is certainly more attractive to leave the two bars different.***

1) ***streng im Takt***
bien en mesure / to coincide precisely with the tact

ffp
pp
ca - - lan - - do
(i. t.)
più p
mp
legato

ff
sf
ben marc.
sf
sf
ff
p
ri
tar
dan
do
dim.
pp
in tempo
mp
un poco risoluto
fp
pp
mp espressivo
sf
Ped.

a) Siehe Seite 5a) b) c).
Voir page 5a) b) c).
Vide page 5a) b) c).

b) Siehe Seite 6 a).
Voir page 6 a).
Vide page 6 a).

a) *Siehe Seite 6 b).* b) *Siehe Seite 6 c).*
Voir page 6 b). *Voir page 6 c).*
Vide page 6 b). *Vide page 6 c).*

LARGO APPASSIONATO (♪ = 69)

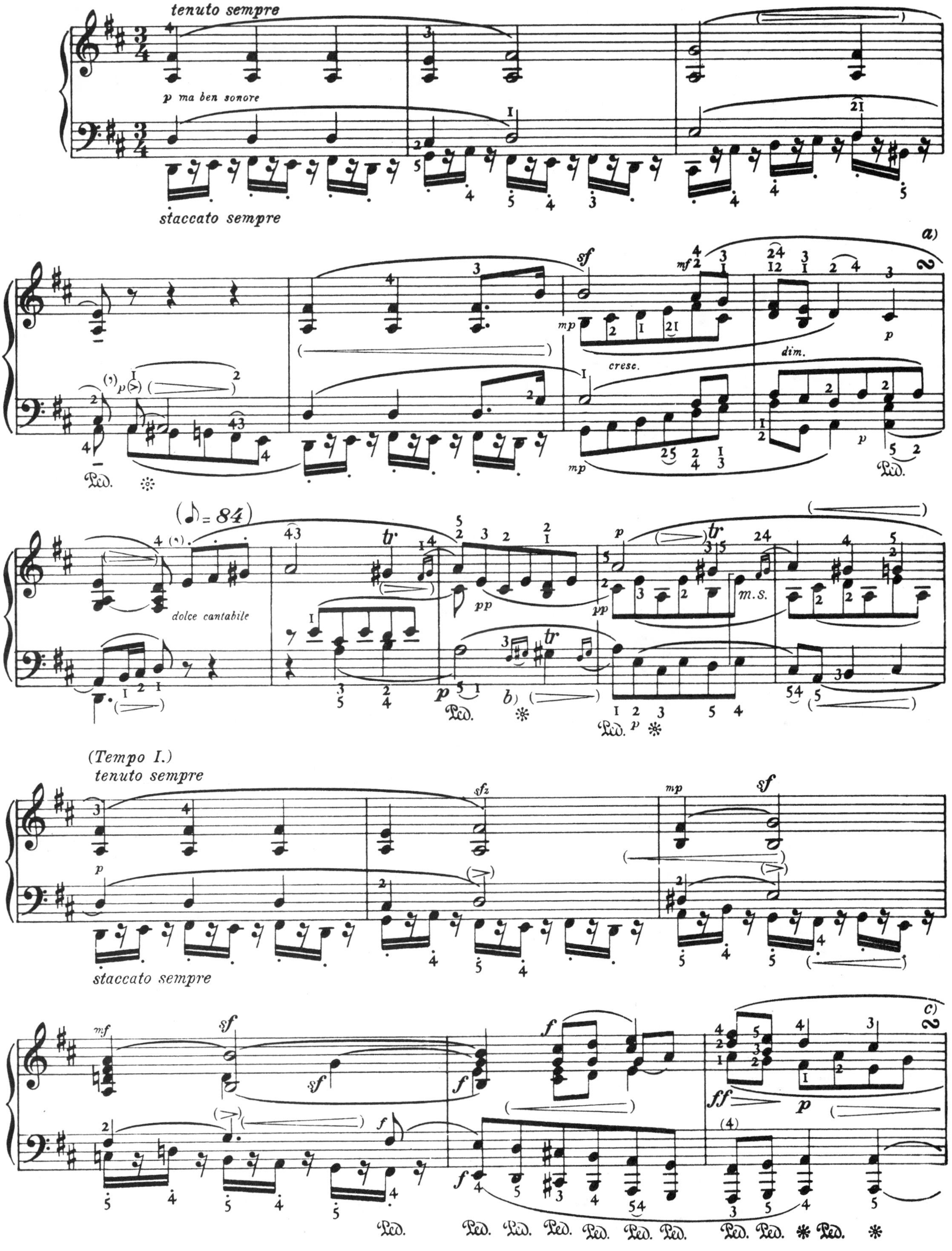
tenuto sempre
p ma ben sonore
staccato sempre
a)
sf
mf
cresc.
dim.
mp
p
(♪ = 84)
dolce cantabile
tr
pp
m.s.
b)
(Tempo I.)
tenuto sempre
sfz
sf
staccato sempre
f
ff
c)

a)
(tranquillo)

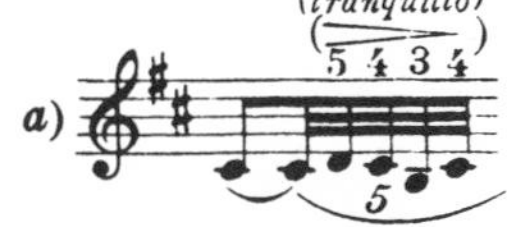

b) Den Vorschlag langsamer als den Nachschlag: etwa wie Zweiunddreißigstel.

b) Prenez l'agrément plus lentement que la note complementaire: à peu près le temps d'une quadruple-croche.

b) Take the appoggiatura slower than the complementary note; about like semidemiquavers.

c)

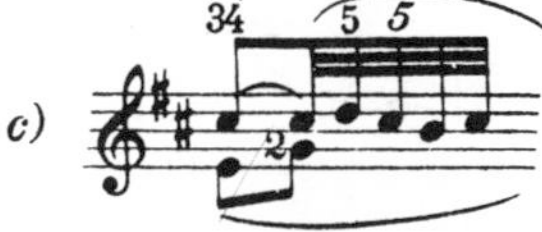

1) innig zart
avec une douce tendresse
tenderly and delicately

a) s. Seite 14 a)
voir page 14 a)
vide page 14 a)

b) s. Seite 14 b)
voir page 14 b)
vide page 14 b)

m.d.
m.s.
poco rit.
Ped.
in tempo primo
tenuto sempre
staccato sempre
un poco più mosso
(Tempo II.)
più p
poco rit.
♪ = 76
in tempo primo, dolcissimo, ma ben cantando
tenuto
staccato

a) Oberer Fingersatz Original von Beethoven | a) le doigté supérieur est de Beethoven | a) the upper fingering is prefixed by Beethoven

f
p
cresc.
f
ff
p
Ped.
rallentando
pp
1
a tempo
p
f
ff
ff
ff
ff

TRIO
Più mosso (𝅗𝅥. = 66)
poco
molto
marcatissimo
Scherzo D. C.
RONDO
GRAZIOSO (𝅗𝅥 = 132)
sempre molto p
dolce

mp
più p
sf
mp
pp
pp
sf
sf
p
p
Ped.
a)
(♩= 144)
dolce
leggiero, melodiosamente
pp
Ped.
Ped.
Ped.
Ped.
Ped.
Ped.
p giocoso
molto leggiero
Ped.

a)

b) Ob der Doppelschlag zwischen drittem und viertem Viertel, ob zwischen siebentem und achtem Achtel auszuführen sei, ist mit Bestimmtheit wohl kaum zu sagen; es sind beide Arten denkbar.

b) Il n'est guere possible de dire avec certitude s'il faut exécuter le battement entre la 3e et la 4e noire „ou entre la 7e et la 8e; les deux façons ne sont pas bien claires.

b) It can hardly be said with some degree of certainty whether the double turn is to be executed between the 3d and 4th crotchet or between the 7th and 8th quaver; both ways are indistinct.

Also entweder: / Il faut jouer: / One can play this way: — oder: / ou bien: / or: — diese zweite Lösung auch so — leichter: / ou bien, en facilitant la dernière manière: / this second way also thus: — or, easier:

oder / ou bien: / or,

Ich spiele die Stelle, je nach Laune, sowohl in der einen, wie in der anderen Weise.
Pour moi, je suis mon caprice en jouant ce passage une fois d'une telle manière, une fois de l'autre.
As for me, I play this passage just as fancy strikes me, the one or the other way.

Tempo I
molto p
più p
v. p. 21 a)
(♩ = 138)

staccato sempre brioso
ff
marcatissimo
sf
staccato
sf
ff

legato
pp subito
pp
sempre p
ff subito
sf
ff

ff
pp subito
(Tempo I)
legierissimo
pp
m. d.
m. s.
senza Ped.
molto p
p
mf

sf
p
m.d.
mp
v. p. 21 a)
(♩= 144)
dolce
Ped.
molto leggiero
v. p. 22 a)

a)
v.p. 22 b)
sf
p
mf
b)
Tempo I
Ped.

tr
tr
v.p. 28 b)
(♩= 138)
mp sempre
più p
dolce
pp
mp
sf
sopra
m.s.
mf
sempre staccato
m.s.
stacc.
f
Ped.

p subito
sempre stacc.
Ped.
f
sf
mf
ff
sfp
decresc.
m. 8.

(♩= 126)
pp
p
molto p
Ped.
rubato
sfp
i.t. dolce, semplice
a)
tranquillo, ma in tempo
mp melodiosamente
sf
p liberamente
tr
sfp
f
tranquillo, ma non rit.
p

SONATE

No. 3

JOSEPH HAYDN GEWIDMET

sf
mf
leggiero, ma mf
tr
meno ff, poco f
ff
Ped.
a)
p

(♩= 160)

a) 1) *allegramente*

b)

dolce

a) *Nach meiner Ansicht f in der rechten Hand erst auf dem zweiten Viertel.*

a) *A mon avis, main droite ne devrait jouer „forte" qu'au 2e temps.*

a) *In my opinion, „forte" in the right hand only upon the second crotchet.*

b) *Die übliche Spielweise ist:*

b) *Manière habituelle d'exécuter ce passage:*

b) *The customary execution is this:*

Der aufgezeichneten Bewegung gemäß, die als zweites Achtel jeder der 3 Figuren gerade die untere Wechselnote verlangt, müßte die Stelle allerdings wie folgt ausgeführt werden:

Si l'on désirait exécuter ce passage conformément au mouvement noté, qui demande pour chacune des 3 figures la note inférieure en appogiature, il faudrait le faire comme suit:

According to the annotated movement which requires exactly the lower appoggiatura as the second quaver of each of the 3 figures, this passage, to be sure, would have to be executed like this:

Wenn ich auch meine, daß diese textgetreue — vielmehr buchstabengetreue — Ausführung durchaus ungezwungen, ja hier sogar besser klingt, als die zuerst angegebene, ist wohl dennoch diese, die verbreitete Lesart, als die richtige anzusehen.

Bien que cette manière textuelle, ou mieux: littérale, d'exécuter le passage me paraisse tout à fait naturelle — et même plus agréable que l'autre dans le cas que voici — je crois que la première manière doit être considérée comme la plus authentique.

In my opinion, this textual — or rather literal — execution sounds absolutely free and easy, here even better than the one first mentioned; — yet this way of reading, which is generally accepted, is to be considered the correct one.

(Obzwar dazu die Aufzeichnung genügt hätte.)

(Il eût d'ailleurs suffi de la noter ainsi:)

(Although, for this execution, the following annotation would have been sufficient:)

Die Entscheidung wird durch die eine Note der Parallelstelle herbeigeführt, die diese von der hier besprochenen unterscheidet: durch das zweite Achtel der zweiten Figur. Dort wird es vom unteren Halbton gebildet: ais. Von ihm zu h Doppelschlag also entweder:

On décidera du choix en comparant ce passage ci au passage parallèle, ou une seule note établit la différence: la seconde croche de la deuxième figure. Dans le passage parallèle, cette note est formée par le demi-ton inférieur: la dièze. On passe au si par le moyen d'un battement, soit:

The decision is brought about by the one note of the parallel passage by which it is distinguished from the one considered here: viz., by the second quaver of the second figure. There it is formed by the lower half tone: a sharp. From this to b double turn; therefore either:

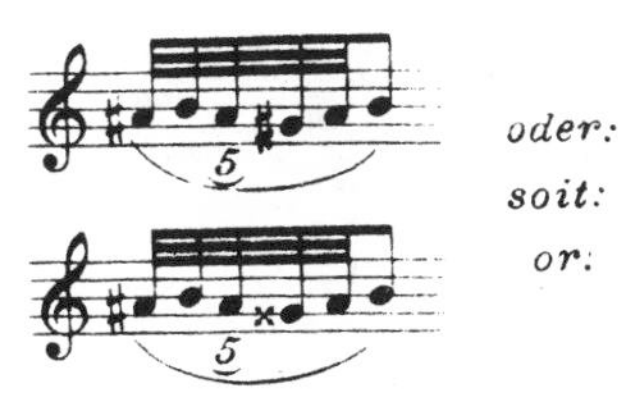

Diese Schritte können kaum gewollt sein; sie klingen in diesem Stück ganz befremdlich und sind zum G-dur-Dreiklang fast undenkbar. Es gibt eine dritte Möglichkeit, nämlich:

Ces mouvements ne peuvent pas avoir été dans l'intention de l'auteur; ils produisent une étrange dissonance dans ce morceau et ne s'harmonisent d'aucune facon avec l'accord de sol majeur. Voici une troisième possibilité:

These movements were certainly not intended by the composer; they sound quite strange in this piece and are almost unthinkable together with the g-major chord. There is a third possibility, viz.: —

1) *frisch, mit Feuer* — *avec feu et entrain* — *lively, with animation*

a)
b)
piu p
cantabile mp
mp
mf
sf
sempre f
Ped.

(♩= 168)
legato
ff
sff Ped.
(♩= 160)
sf
p
a)
tr
pp
pmp
f
Ped.
ff
1.
2.
(2)
a)

v. p. 7a)
s. S. 7a)
pp
p
pp
f
ff
sf Ped.
sf Ped.
sf Ped.
sf Ped.
sf
calando
dim.
mf Ped.
Ped.
Ped.
Ped.
(♩= 152)
in tempo
pp

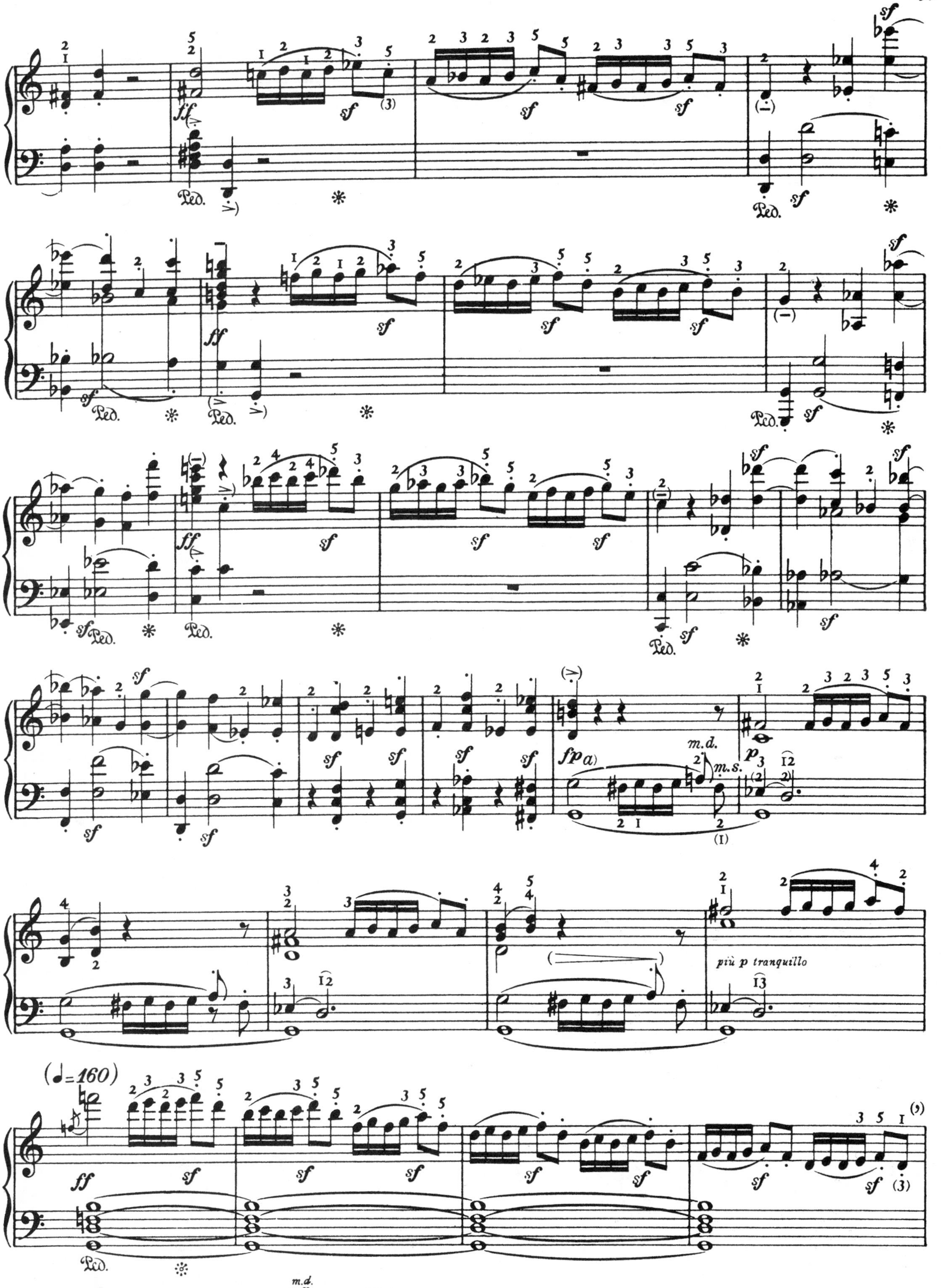
Ped.
fp a)
m.d.
m.s.
più p tranquillo
(♩=160)

a) Leichtere Ausführung:
Exécution plus facile:
Easier of execution:

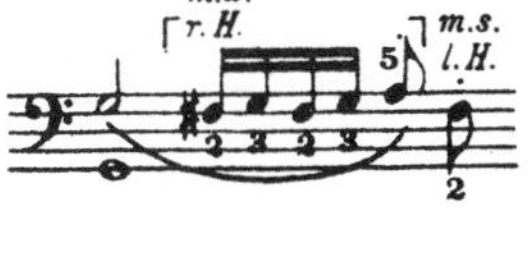
m.d.
r.H.
m.s.
l.H.

(Tempo I)
poco f
leggiero, ma mf
Ped.

allegramente (𝅗𝅥 = 160)
dolce

v. p. 6a)
più p
mp cantabile
mp
mf
sf
sempre f
Ped.
legato
(♩= 168)

(♩= 160)
v.p. 7 a)
s.S. 7a)
sempre molto pp
Ped.

a) Fermate nicht zu lang etwa drei Viertel Klang, zwei Viertel Luftpause.
b) Etwa vier Viertel.
c) *f* etwa fünf Achtel wert, der chromatische Lauf drei.

a) Ne prolongez pas le temps de repos outremesure: à peu près 3 noires de repos sur la touche et une pause de 2 noires.
b) Temps de repos d'à peu près 4 noires.
c) Repos d'à peu près 5 croches; le passage chromatique completa 3 croches.

a) Don't lengthen the fermata too much; about three crotchets sound, two crotchets air interval.
b) About four crotchets.
c) About 5 quaver's worth; the chromatic run, three.

(Tempo I)
(♩= 168)
p
mp
vivace
ff subito
p
pp
1
ff
ff
ff

1) mit inniger Empfindung
tendre
fervently

espr. ma molto dolce
più espr., poco rubato, ma sempre dolce
pp
più p
dim. poco calando
molto p
semplice
sopra
p espr.
poco
cre
scendo
Ped. simile
poco rit.
ten.
molto
i.t.
sempre espr.
Ped. simile
più intensivo
mp
mf
molto p
dim.

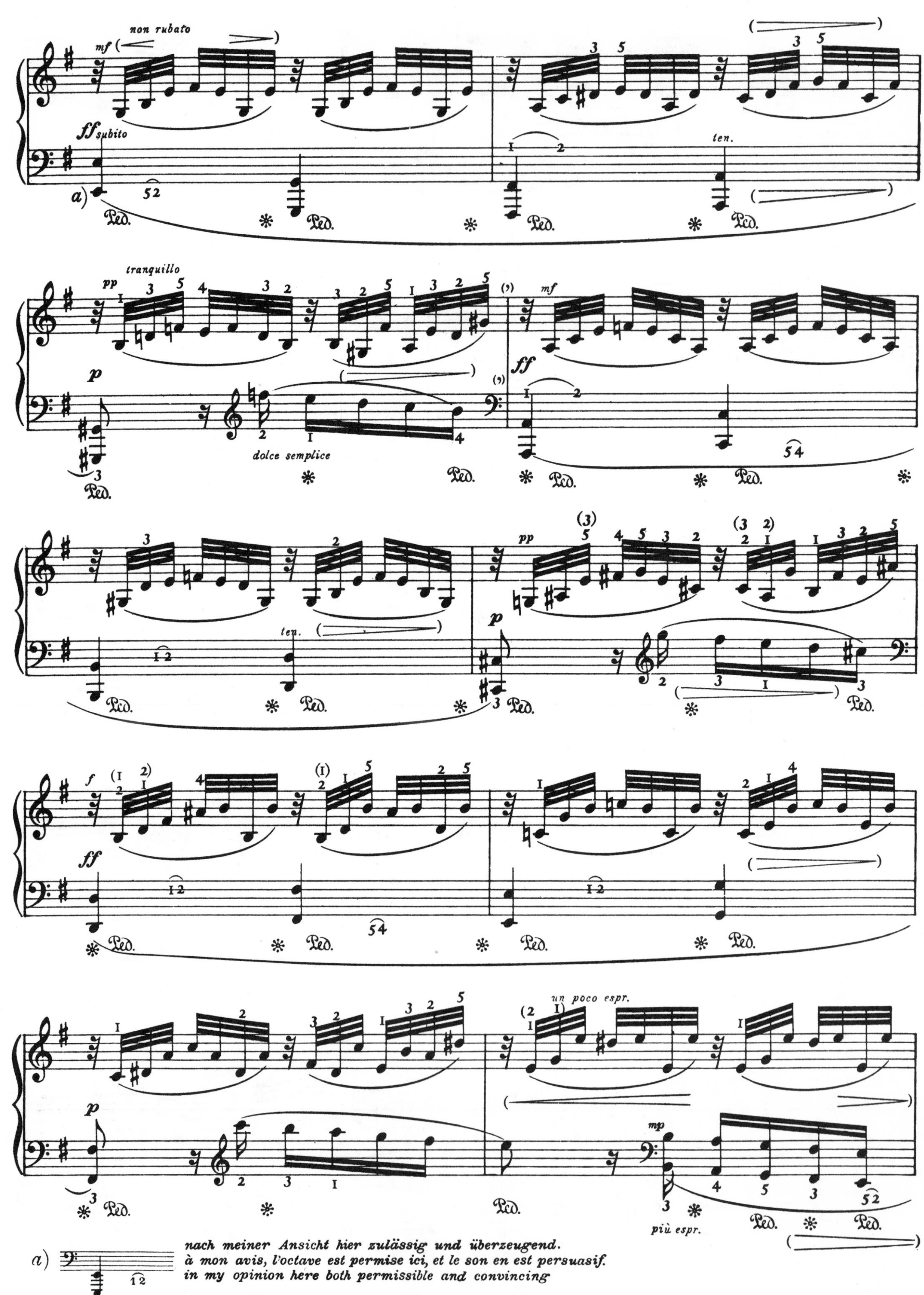

a) nach meiner Ansicht hier zulässig und überzeugend.
à mon avis, l'octave est permise ici, et le son en est persuasif.
in my opinion here both permissible and convincing

p dolce
molto dolce, espr.
meno pp
ten.
non troppo
smorz.
(Tempo I)
un poco calando
p dolce
Ped.

1) *erhaben*
avec grandeur
lofty

2) *mit aller Innerlichkeit*
très tendre
fervently

meno sf
f subito
liberamente
quieto
a)
b)

SCHERZO

Allegro **(♩. = 104)**

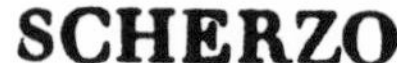

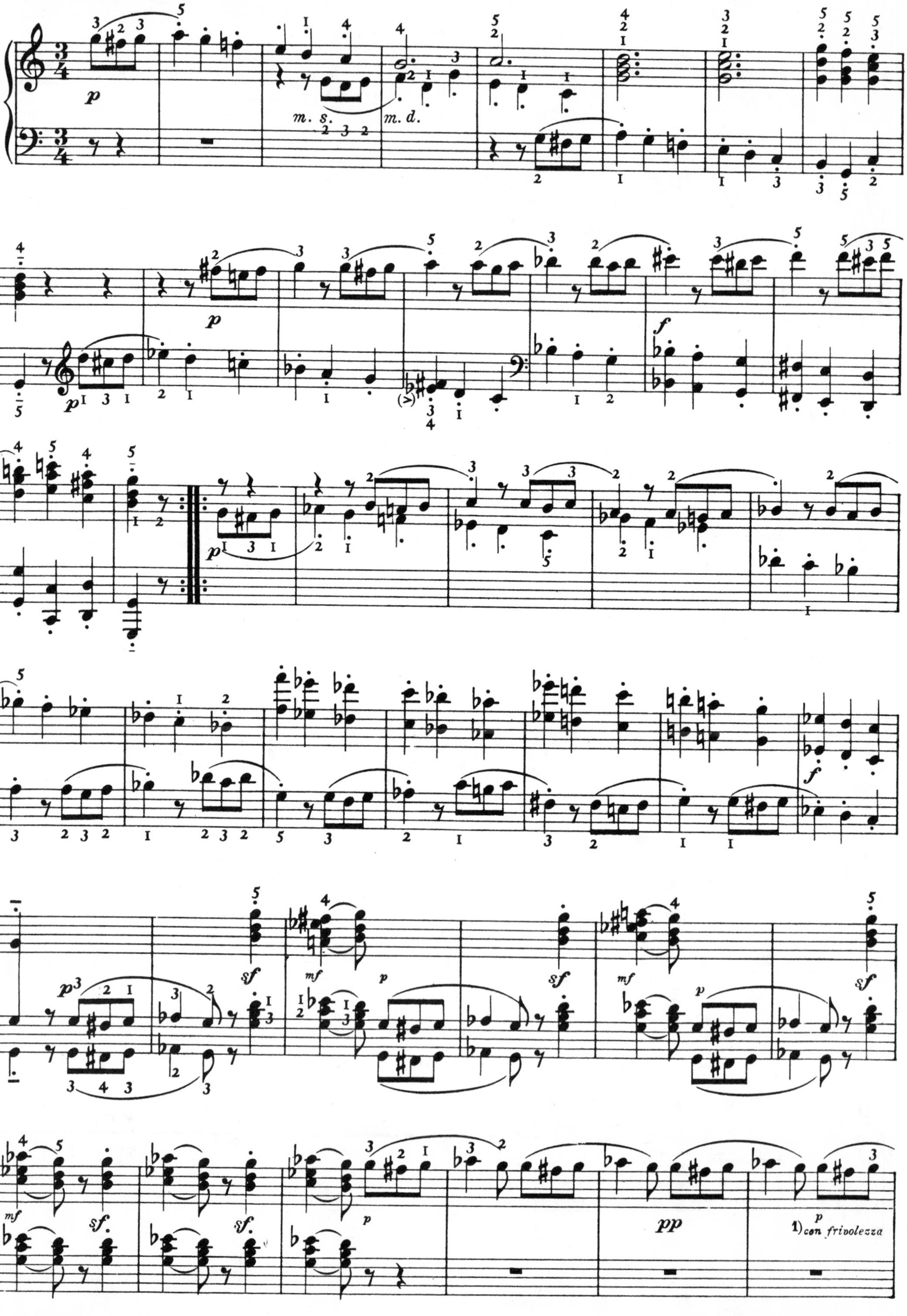

p
m. s.
m. d.
f
sf
mf
pp
1) con frivolezza

1) *etwas leichtfertig im Charakter*
d'une manière un peu libre et dégagée
somewhat free and easy

m. s. m. d.

TRIO (𝅗𝅥. = 96)

non legato

p, ma ben marc.

molto leggiero

piu p

mp(> poco
sf
p leggiero
mp
cresc.
f
(> poco

1) nicht beschleunigen
sans accélérer le mouvement
don't accelerate

1) und so fort
et caetera
and so on

1) liebenswürdig
aimable
pleasantly, coaxingly

f meno legato
m.s.
m.d.
p molto legato
sf p
pp
f
ff
p

1) *fließend*
d'un mouvement fluide
fluently

2) *Oberstimme*
la voix superieure
upper voice

p dolce cantabile
p
pp
sf
dolce
p cantabile
più p

pp
sf
p
sfp
sf
p
sfp
sfp
sfp
più p
pp
f
f

1) heiter 2) kräftig, keck.
gai avec vigueur et entrain
gaily with dash and vigour

p subito
poco
più p
p
poco
p
p
p

m.d.
m. s.
sf
p
sf
p
sfp
13
tr
ff
14
p
21
tr

crescendo
Ped.
p subito
sempre p
diminuendo
p subito
pp
calando
p dolce
staccato
più p
rallentando
staccato
Tempo primo
ff

SONATE

No. 4

DER GRÄFIN BABETTE VON KEGLEVICS GEWIDMET

ALLEGRO MOLTO E CON BRIO (♩. = 132) **BEETHOVEN, Op. 7**

a) *Ein weiterer Fingersatz:* 345 | 545454 | 5453 usf. | a) *Autre doigté:* 345 | 545454 | 5453 etc. | a) *Another way of fingering:* 345 | 545454 | 5453 etc.

sf
Ped.
p
ff
a)
sf Ped.
un poco meno forte
sempre marcatissimo
etc.

più f
più ff
ff
fp
più p
mp
sf
Ped.

sf
ff
p
decresc.
pp
Ped.
p

a) *Siehe Seite 6 a)*
Voir page 6 a)
vide page 6 a)

sf
sf
p
sf
cresc.
ff
pp
Ped.

meno
mf
sf
Ped.
p
ff
poco
cresc.

a) *Siehe Seite 6a)*
Voix page 6a)
vide page 6a)

sf
sf
sf
Ped.
più f
sf
ff
più ff
ff
ff
ff
ff
p
sopra
cresc.

f
ff
sf
pp
più pp
tranquillo
p
molto dolce
un poco espr.
i.t.
cresc.
più ff

LARGO, CON GRAN ESPRESSIONE (♪ = 72—80)
sonore
cantabile
molto p
ten.
rinf.
cresc.
pp
ff
fp
sfp
sf
Ped.

pp
pp
p espr.
sempre tenuto
con calore
p cantabile
sempre staccato e pianissimo
sf
sfp
f
f
sempre staccato
p
tenuto
p cantabile
pp
pp staccato
f
sf cresc.
cresc.
sf
f
f
pp

a) *Siehe Seite 15a)*
Voir page 15a)
vide page 15a)

dolce
poco
più
rinf.
sf
sfp
pp
ff
f
p
molto p
cantabile
mp
a)

più espr.

ben in tempo

semplice

1) come una dimanda

simile

2) di tutto cuore

a)

molto quieto

largo

b)

a) b)

1) wie eine Frage.
en interrogeant
as if questioning

2) mit aller Empfindung.
avec ferveur
fervently

ALLEGRO (𝅗𝅥. = 69)
p dolce
Ped.
mp
pp
p
sf
mf
f
poco

tr
mp
più
mancando
pp
(i.t.)
p
dolce
Ped.
decresc.

cresc.
f
ff
sf
sf
sf
sf
sf
f
Ped.
1.
2.
MINORE (𝅗𝅥. = 76)
pp
ffp
ffp

molto
p
decresc.
Ped.
pp
p
ffp
ffp
f

p subito
Ped.
ffp
ffp
sf
sf
ff
pp
più pp
quieto
ppp
Allegro D.C.

RONDO

Poco Allegretto e grazioso (♩=69)

1) *frisch*
avec vivacite
lively

1) fein und anmutig.
avec grâce et finesse
subtle and graceful

a) Siehe Seite 25a)
Voir page 25a)
vide page 25a)

1.
2.
sf
ff

ff
sf
f
m.d.
m.s.
Ped.

a) Siehe Seite 25a)
Voir page 25a)
vide page 25a)

b) Siehe Seite 25b)
Voir page 25b)
vide page 25b)

a) Siehe Seite 25 a)
Voir page 25 a)
Vide page 25 a)

a) Leichtere Ausführung: Exécution plus facile: This way is easier of execution.

b) Siehe Seite 27 b) Voir page 27 b) Vide page 27 b)

a) Siehe Seite 25 a)
Voir page 25 a)
Vide page 25 a)

b) Siehe Seite 25 b)
Voir page 25 b)
Vide page 25 b)

crescendo
Ped.
sfz
legato, sempre simile
cresc.
semplice e tranquillo
decrescendo
pp

SONATE

No. 5

DER GRÄFIN VON BROWNE GEWIDMET

ALLEGRO MOLTO E CON BRIO (𝅗𝅥. = 76–88) **BEETHOVEN, Op. 10 Nr. 1**

a) oder: / ou bien: / or: — die Ausführung: / l'exécution: / this way of executing: — halte ich für unrichtig. / me paraît fausse. / seems to me to be wrong.

cresc.
non legato
leggiero
cresc. molto
semplice
poco
più p
meno

cantanbile, dolce
sempre ben legato e
molto p
sempre col ped. simile
a)
un poco più p
senza ped.
pp
p cresc.
sf
p
cresc.
f

a) Manche Ausgaben haben hier as statt c. | a) Dans quelques éditions on trouve ici la♭ au lieu de do (d'ut) | a) Some editions have here a flat instead of c.

p, dolce cantabile
fp
pp
p
Ped.
dolce cantando
piu p, leggiero
leggiero, non legato
a)
b)
sf
f subito

a) v. p. 4 b)

cresc.
cresc.
Ped.
fp leggiero
p cresc. molto
poco fp
più p
meno fp

Adagio molto (♪ = 63)
a)
b)
mp
cresc.
fp
Ped.
35
tr
più p
dolcissimo
pp
dolce, cantando
p
dolce
poco cresc.
f
c)
molto pp
a)
b) come a.
c)

a)
leggiero
sempre pp
Ped.
cresc.
b)
sf
p
pp
rinf
sostenuto
i.t.
rinf subito

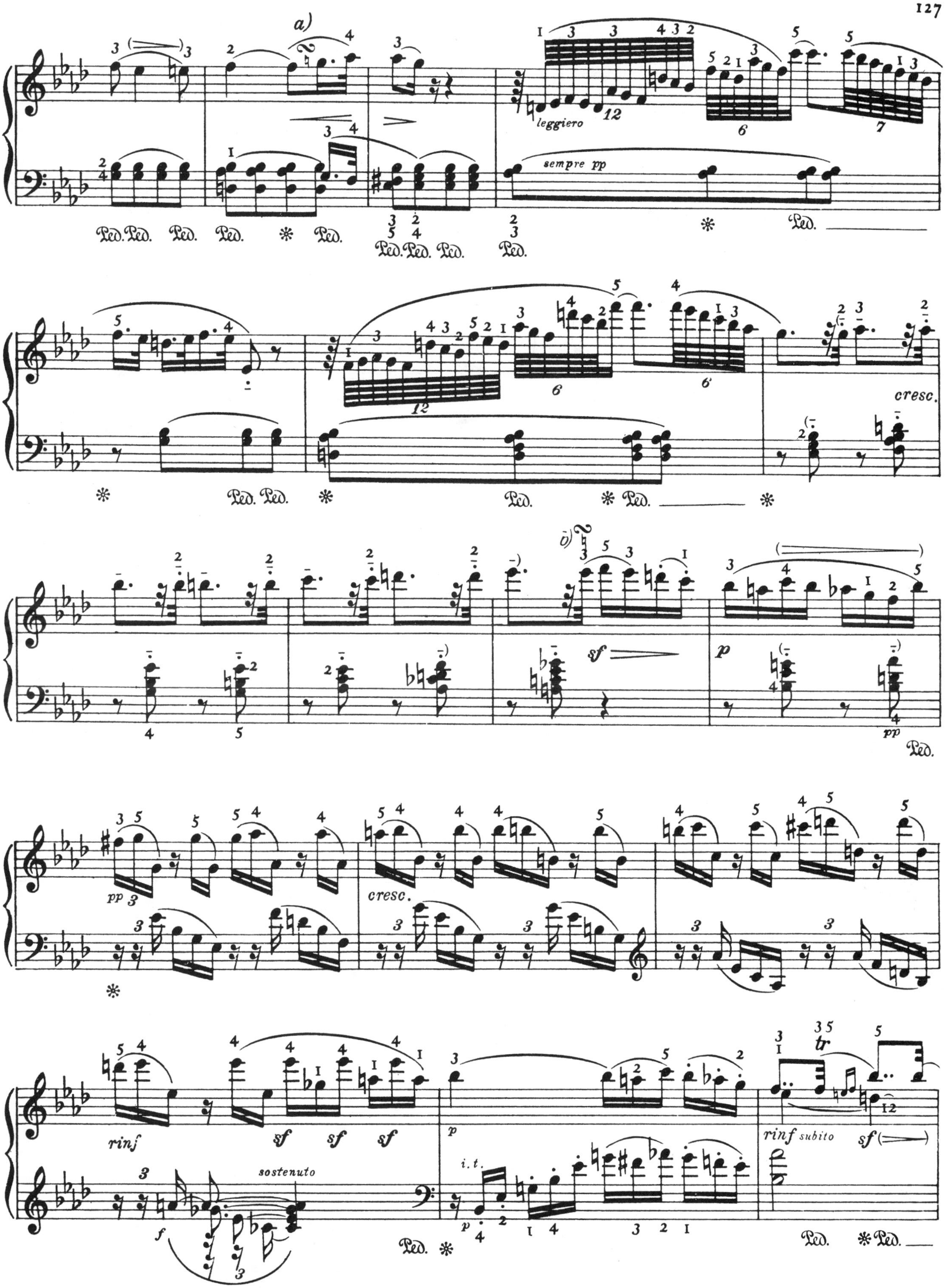

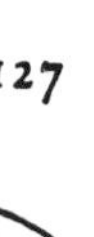

a) v.p.10c).

b)

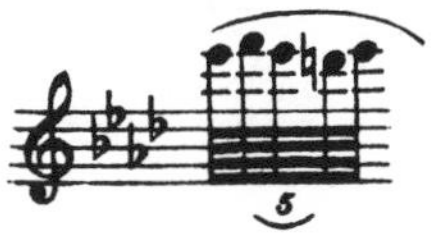

rinf
sfp
Ped.
ff
cresc.
sf
più p
ben tranquillo
dolce
poco

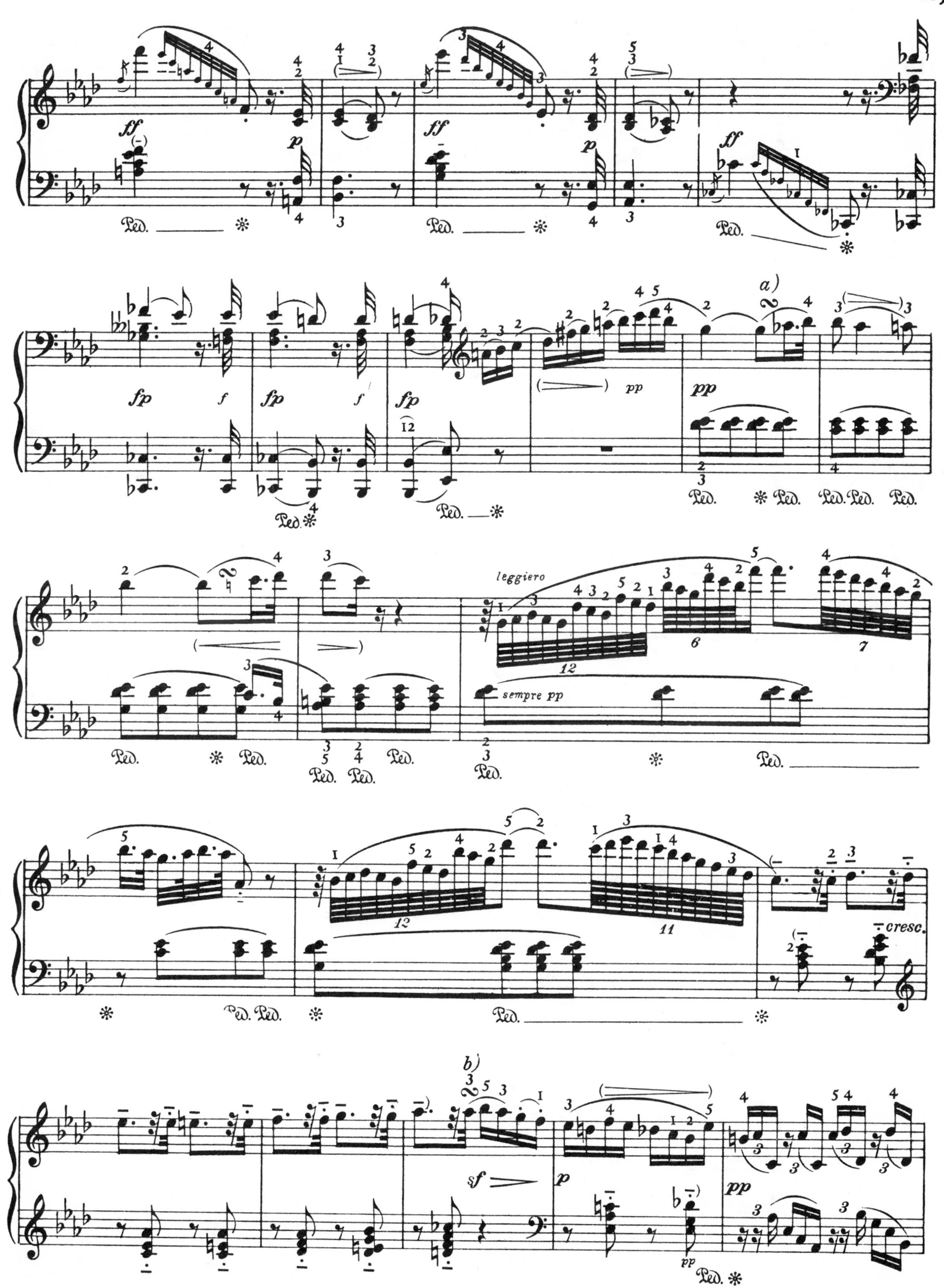

a) v.p. 10 c   b) v.p. 11 b

cresc.
rinf
sf
sostenuto
Ped.
i.t.
p
rinf subito sf
f
rinf
sf p
cantabile, con sentimento
a)
Ped. simile
pp
de - cre - scen - do
pp
a)

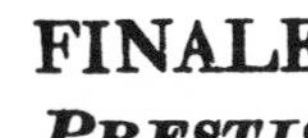

FINALE

PRESTISSIMO (𝅗𝅥 = 104—112)

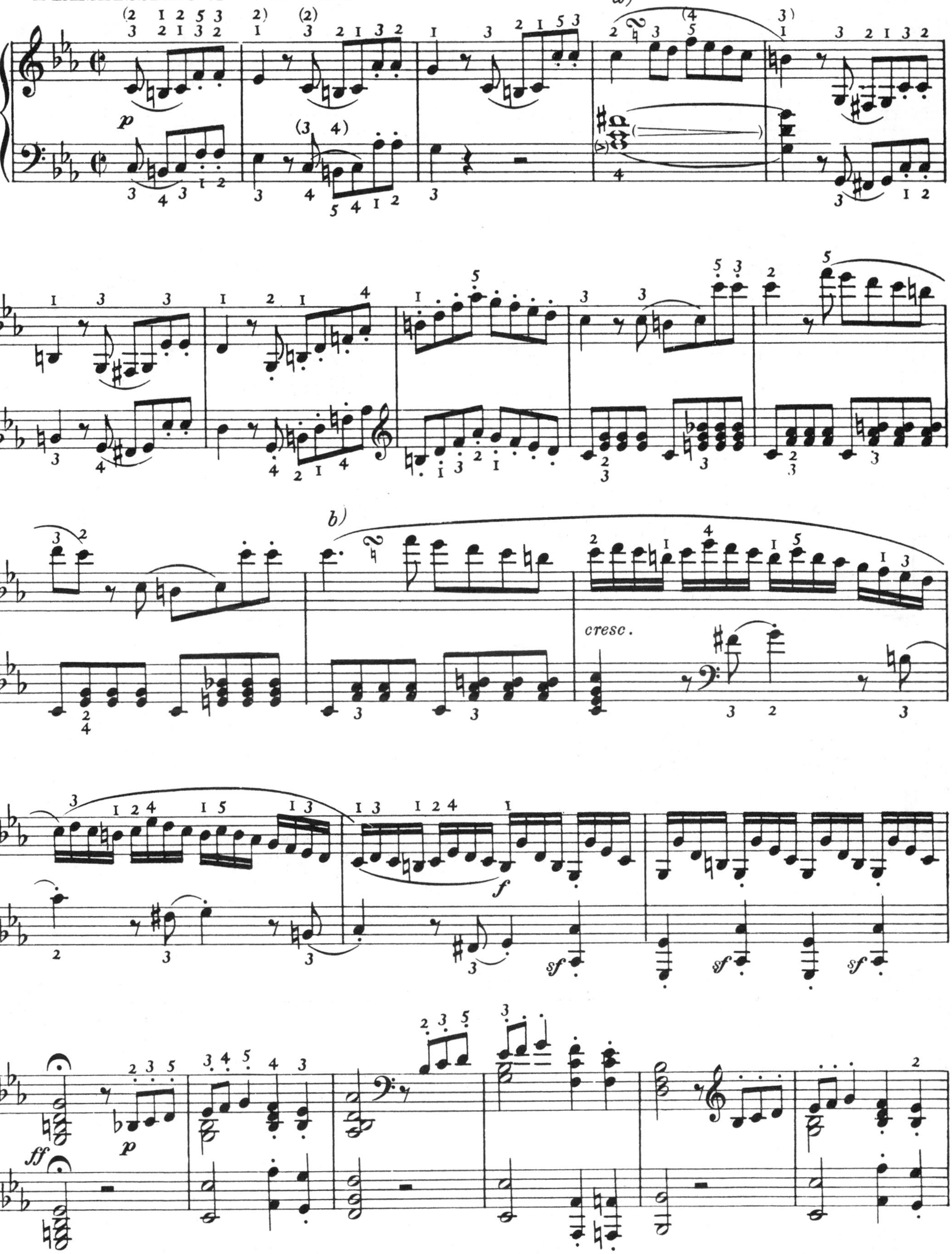
a)
b)
cresc.

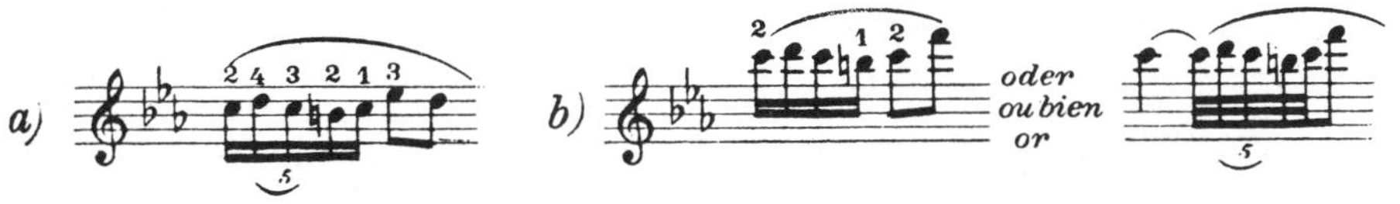
a)
b)
oder
ou bien
or

ff [p]
fp
Ped.
cresc.
ff
p
sf

p
sf
cresc.
ff
marcatissimo
sopra
sopra
senza rit.
sf
sf
p
cresc.
f
sf
sf
sf
[ff]
p

ffp
Ped.
fp
cresc.
sf
ff
p

ff
ff
p
Ped.
cresc.
fp
pp
p ri - tar - dan - do
ca - lan - do
tenuto
Adagio
rp
tenuto
Tempo I
ff
p
decresc.
pp
Ped.

SONATE

No. 6

DER GRÄFIN VON BROWNE GEWIDMET

ALLEGRO (𝅗𝅥 = 104)

BEETHOVEN, Op. 10 Nr. 2

cresc.
staccato

sopra
tr
Ped.
cresc.
sffz
ff
p
f
mf
a)

fp
Ped.
cresc.
fp
Ped.
cresc.
ff
fp
Ped.
cresc.
Ped.
p

p cresc.
f
p
cresc.
f
ff
ff
sf
sf
decresc.
p
pp

p
Ped.
pp
mp
p cresc.
sf
Ped. simile

pp
p
sf
f
ff
pp
a)

pp
cresc.
f
sf
f
ff
ff
p
sopra
f
f
p
f
sffz
mf
sfz
cresc.
mf
sffz
ff
1.
2.
Ped.

ALLEGRETTO (𝅗𝅥. = 66)
espr.
mp poco espr.
mp, ma dolce
poco
piu p
p semplice

dolcissimo e tranquillo
a)
cresc.
non dim.
senza Ped.
cresc.
oder
ou
or,

a) v. p. 11a)

cresc.
f
p
non legato
sf
f sf
pp
ppp
mp
rf
p
p, ma sonore
più p
fp
cresc.
non stringere
f marc.

1) ohne Hast
sans hâte
no hurry!

2) deutlichst
très distinctement
very distinct!

leggiero
f ben ritmico e marcato
marc.
marc.

sf
p
f
leggierissimo
cresc.
ff
non legato
meno ff

ff
meno ff
ff
non legato
p
cresc.
sempre crescendo poco a poco
f

ff
sf
sf
sf
leggierissimo
p subito
sempre staccatissimo
più p
poco
pp
cresc.
non stringere
ff
marc.

SONATE

No. 7

DER GRÄFIN VON BROWNE GEWIDMET

PRESTO (𝅗𝅥 = 152—168)

BEETHOVEN. Op. 10 Nr. 3

a) Viele Ausgaben haben im ganzen Takt Oktaven

a) Dans beaucoup d'éditions, la mesure tout entière est formée d'octaves.

a) Many editions have octaves throughout the whole bar.

più p, leggiero
pp
p
sf
mp
più p
cresc.
sf
sf
ff
molto
mp
p
Ped.
cresc.
f
tr
a)
p
f
p
poco
più p
p

a)

a)
p
più p
p
più p
pp
cresc.
f
sempre
cresc.
mf
ff
fp
a)

fp
cresc.
ff
pp
piu pp
p
sopra
pp
p
cresc.
ff
ffp
ffp

ff
sf
sf
sf
ff
sf
sf
sf
ff
ff
meno ff
ff
ff

(>)
meno f
cresc.
ff
cresc.
non lunga
sf
p
sf
p
cresc.
sf
sf
sf
sf
sf
ff

Ped.
più p, leggiero
sf
pp
mp
più p
cresc.
ff
molto
mp
p
sf
cresc.
ff
tr
a)
f
p
a)

poco
piu p
p
a)
p
piu p
p
sf
sf
p
pp
cresc.
sf
sf
sf
f
p
sf
cresc.
sf
sf
sf
f
p
sf
sfp
p
cresc.
sf
sempre
sf
cresc.
sf
sf
col 8ra...
a)

ff
col 8va
fp
fp
cresc.
ff
pp
cresc.
f
pp
pp
sf
più pp
sopra
pp

sf
cresc.
p
f
ff
sffz

LARGO E MESTO (♪ = 63)
più p, dolce
cantabile
cresc.
cresc.
espressivo
Ped. Ped.
Ped.
Ped.
sempre legatissimo
cresc.
più espr.
a)
b)

cresc.
ben cantando
ben cantando
dolce
dolce
cresc.

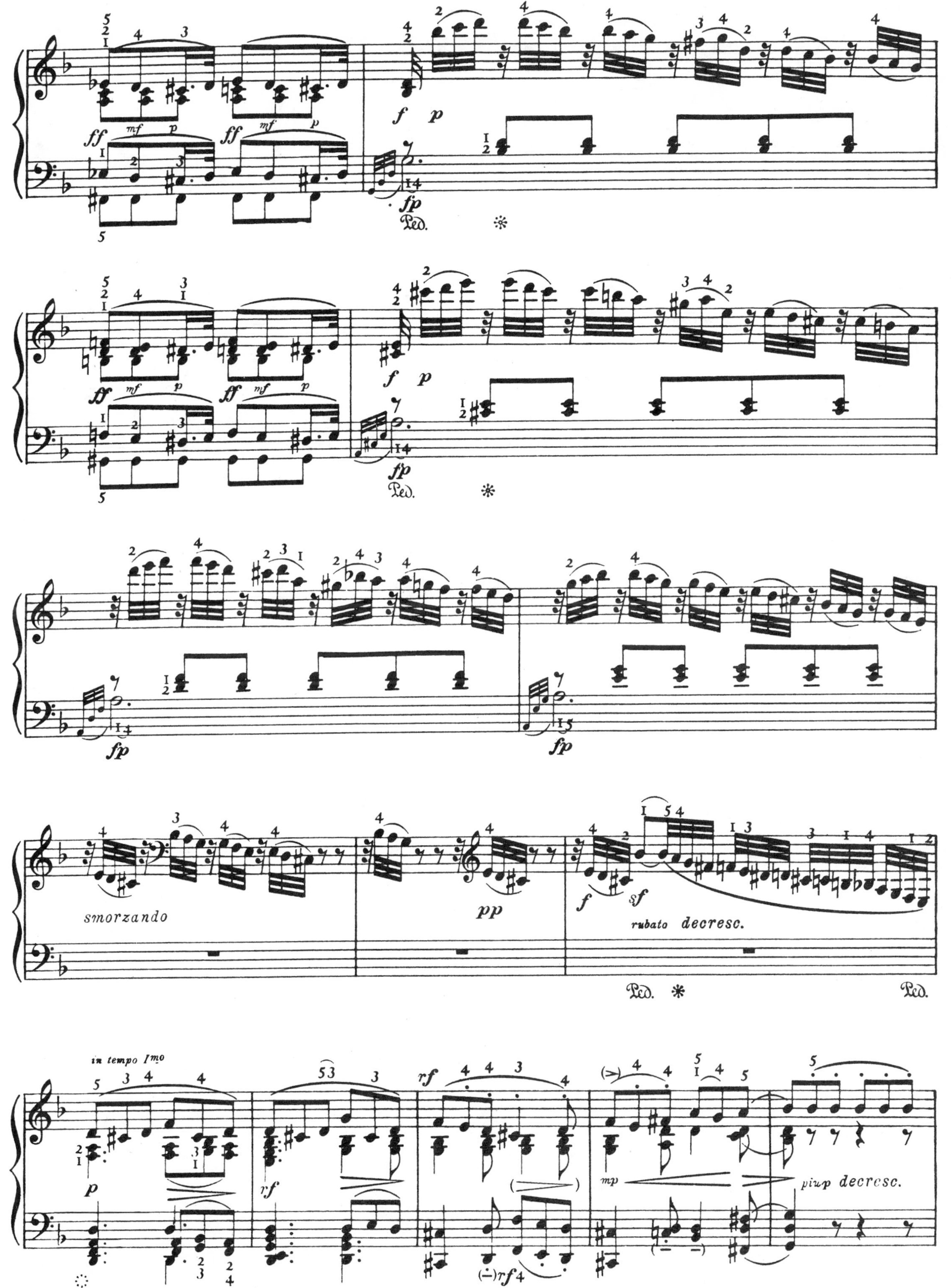
smorzando
pp
rubato decresc.
in tempo Imo
più p decresc.

b) Siehe Seite 13 b.
voir page 13 b
vide page 13 b.

p
pp
cresc.
f
sf
sf
sf
sf
cresc.

MENUETTO

ALLEGRO (𝅗𝅥. = 92–100)

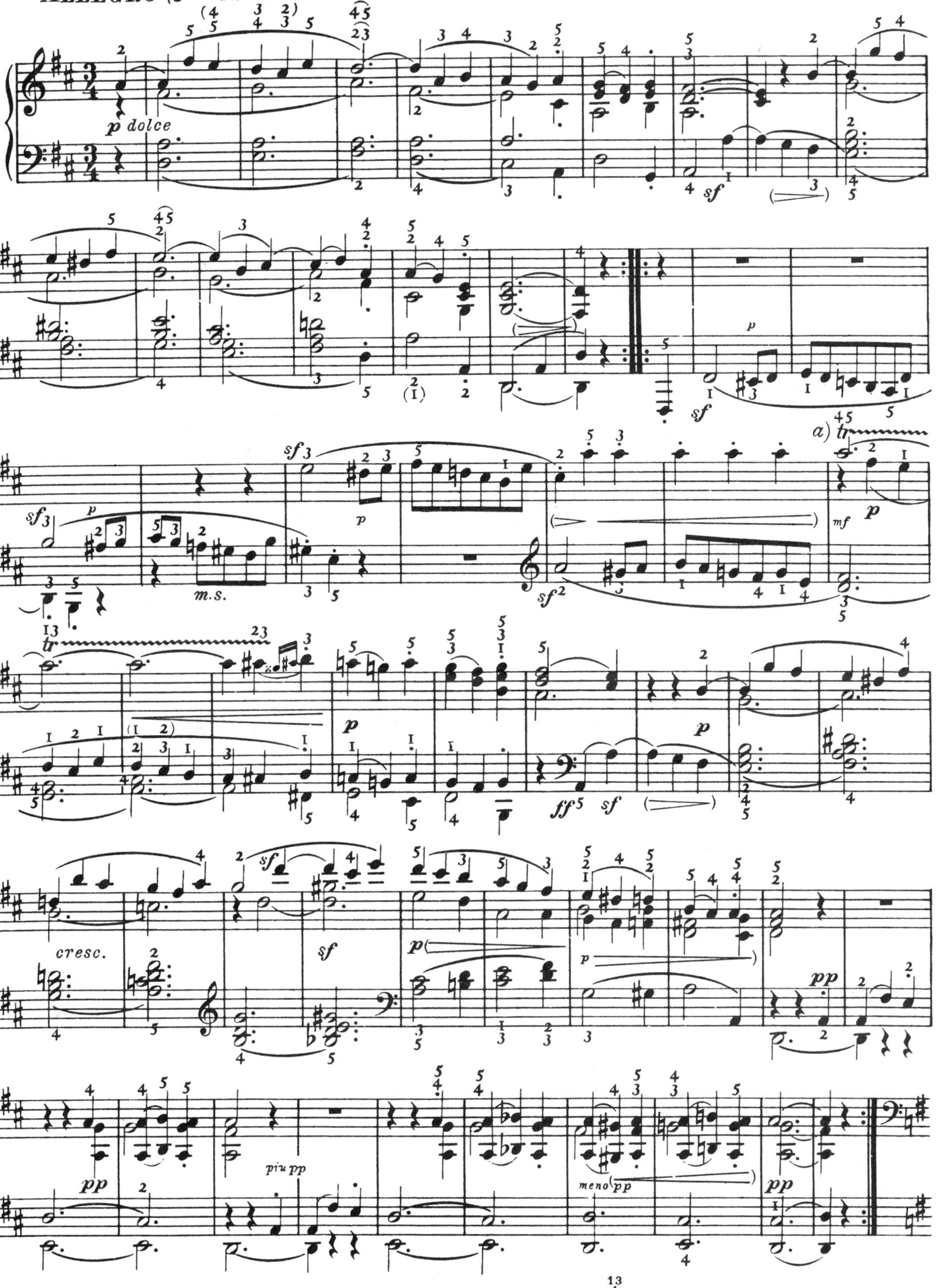
p dolce
sf
p
sf
a) tr
m.s.
mf
tr
ff
cresc.
pp
piu pp
meno pp

a) 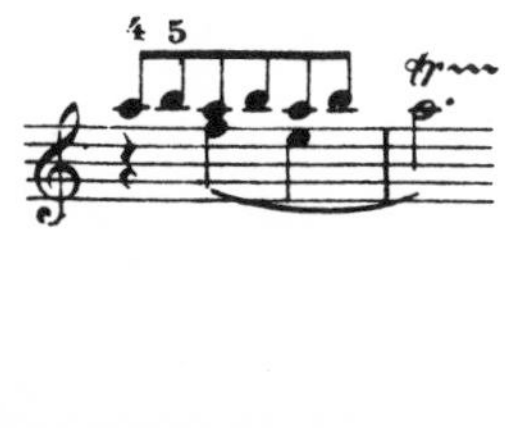

leichter aber in folgender Ausführung:
l'exécution suivante est plus facile:
easier of execution this way:

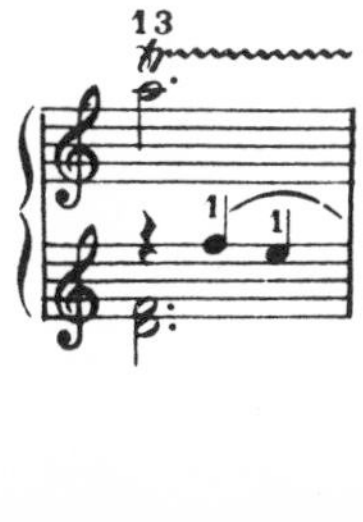

TRIO

(Meno mosso 𝅗𝅥. = 80)

Men. D. C. ma senza replica.

RONDO
ALLEGRO (𝅗𝅥 = 144)
cresc.
cresc.
cresc.
cresc.
leggierissimo
Ped.

cresc.
ff
sf
p
Ped.
cresc.
f
p
pp
ff
p
sf p
leggiero
sf

ff
decresc.
p
pp
sf
cresc.
f

cresc.
p
ff
p
sf
sf
cresc.

più p
legg.
cresc.
cresc.
cresc.

pp
p
cresc.
mf
p
f
ff
sopra
a)
ff
sempre f, energico
sf
ff
Ped.
a)

p
pp
più pp
pp
un poco calando
ppp
i.t., ma ben tranquillo
leggierissimo
pp non pressare
Ped.
poco
dim.
pp
quieto
senza Ped.

SONATE

No. 8

PATHÉTIQUE

DEM FÜRSTEN CARL VON LICHNOWSKY GEWIDMET

GRAVE (♪ = 52)

BEETHOVEN, Op. 13

a) *Etwa sieben Zweiunddreißigstel lang.* | a) *d'une durée d'environ 7 quadruples-croches.* | a) *about 7 demisemiquavers long.*

ALLEGRO DI MOLTO E CON BRIO (𝅗𝅥 = 168–176)

b) Nach der Urtextausgabe. Die meisten Ausgaben haben: Die Parallelstelle, die modulatorisch anders verläuft, kann zur Begründung des zugefügten: C^2 nicht herangezogen werden.

b) Conforme à l'édition originale. La plupart des éditions ont Le passage correspondant, d'une autre modulation, ne peut servir de comparaison justificative pour l'adjonction du do à la quatrième octave.

b) As in the original-text edition. The majority of editions have: There is no justifiable reason for adding the C^2 by quoting the parallel passage, for this modulates differently.

a) Manche haben: „p" schon zum ersten Viertel.
b) Fermate etwa 5 Halbe; keine Luftpause danach.
c) Fermate etwa 7 Halbe; danach 2 Halbe Luftpause (selbstverständlich ohne Pedal.)

a) Certains éditeurs placent le „p" déjà au premier temps.
b) Point d'orgue d'une durée d'environ la valeur de cinq blanches; ne faire suivre d'aucune pause.
c) Point d'orgue d'une durée d'environ la valeur de sept blanches; faire suivre d'un arrêt correspondant à la valeur de deux blanches (évidemment sans prendre de pédale.)

a) Some editions have "p" on the first crotchet.
b) Pause about 5 minims; no breathing-pause afterwards.
c) Pause about 7 minims, then 2 minims breathing-pause (naturally without pedal.)

1) einfach, ängstlich / simple, craintif / simply, anxiously. 2) streng im Takt / bien en mesure / strictly in time. 3) deutlich / distinctement / distinctly.

a) Fermate etwa 5 Achtel lang; keine Luftpause danach. | a) Point d'orgue d'une durée d'environ la valeur de cinq croches, ne faire suivre d'aucune pause. | a) Pause about 5 quavers long; no breathing-pause afterwards.

pp cresc.
Ped.
sf
f
pp
pp
cresc.
Ped.
sf
f
sf
più f
sf
non presto, ben in misura
fp non troppo legato
più p
pp
più pp
tranquillo, ma senza rit.
p
p sfz
cresc.
molto
p

sfz
p
cresc.
Ped.
Ped. simile
p cresc.
sopra
al basso
leggierissimo
pp
sf
più p, leggiero
mf
sf energico
decresc.
f

a) v.p.5a)

un poco calmare
i.t. semplice, quieto
legato
p dolce
pp
legato
marc. non stringere
cresc.
un poco agitato
p legato
f
marc.
cresc.
mp

a) Fermate etwa 7 Halbe; danach Pedal aufheben.

b) Fermate beachten!

a) Point d'orgue d'environ la valeur de sept blanches; lever ensuite la pédale.

b) Tenir compte du point d'orgue.

a) Pause about 7 minims long, then raise the pedal.

b) Observe the pause!

ADAGIO CANTABILE (♪ = 60)
p
pp
p legatissimo ed egualmente
molto p
un poco più sonore
dolcissimo
non secco
Ped.
teneramente, ma sempre dolcissimo
p
pp
sempre legatissimo
pp
moltop
ppp
dolcissimo
p
tranquillo
simile
pp
a)
a)
oder
ou bien
or,

b) Bei Manchen fehlt das „d" im Akkord des vierten Achtels.
b) A l'accord au quatrième temps, il manque parfois le rè.
b) Sometimes the d in the chord of the fourth quaver is missing.
c) Die Gabel fehlt bei Einigen.
c) Certains éditeurs omettent le soufflet.
c) Some omit the cresc. fork.

1) eindringlich
avec un sentiment intense
intense

2) andächtig
dévotement
devoutly

a) Die kritisch durchgesehene Ausgabe hat hier, und ebenso im folgenden Takt auf dem ersten Achtel das Zeichen *rf*. In der „Urtext"ausgabe steht es hingegen nicht.

a) Ici, de même qu'à la mesure suivante, l'édition critique revue place le signe *rf* a la première croche de la mesure. Ce *rf* fait défaut dans l'édition du «texte original.»

a) The critically revised edition has here as well as in the following bar the mark "*rf*" upon the first quaver; in the original text edition there is no such mark.

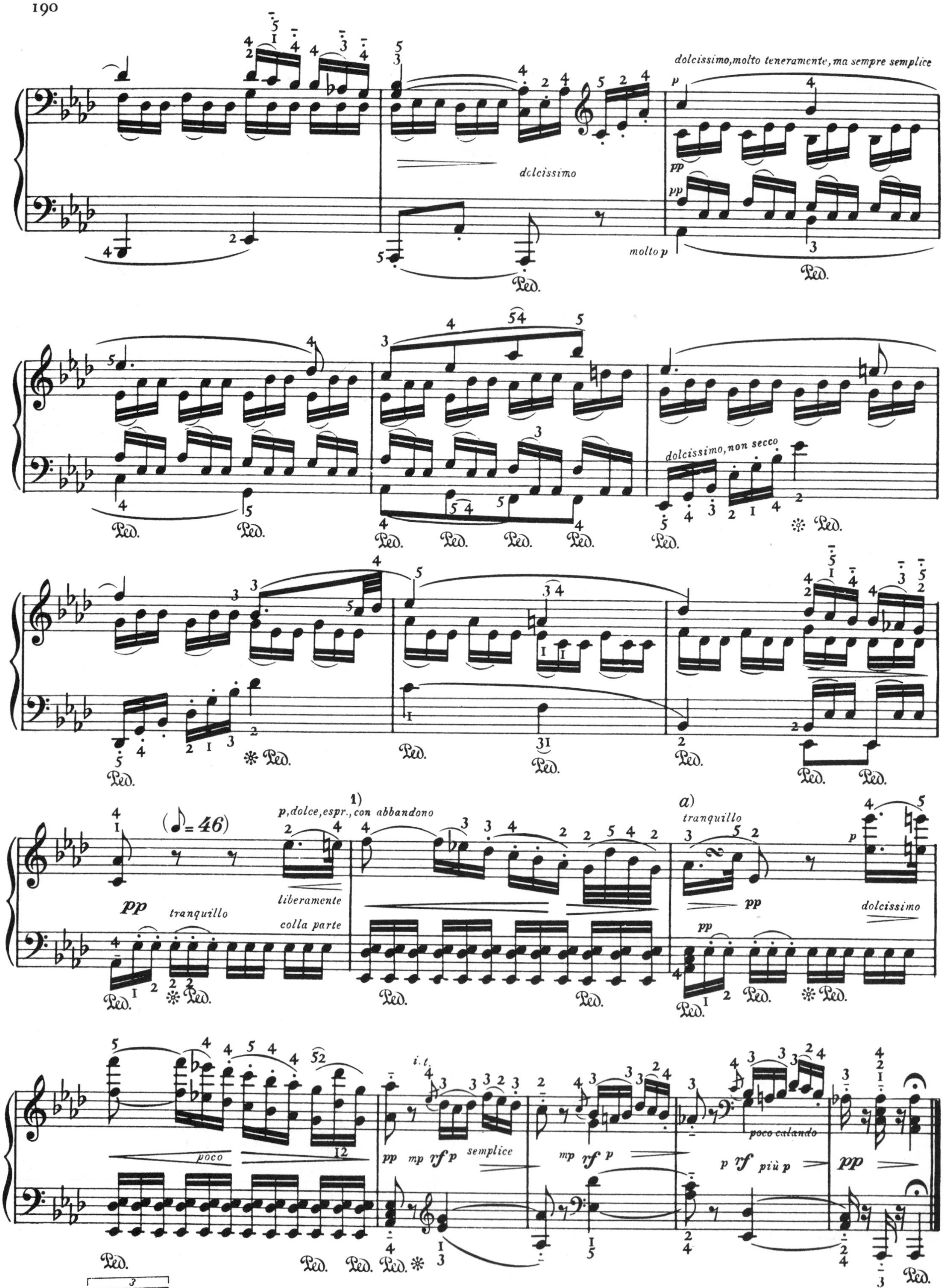

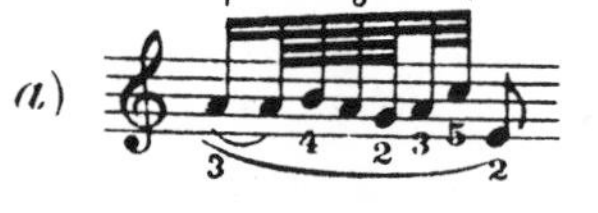

1) hingegeben
avec abandon
unrestrainedly

RONDO

Allegro (𝅗𝅥 = 108)

1) liebenswürdig, gefällig
aimable et gracieux
pleasantly, gracefully

a) Manche haben das Zeichen: *sf* zum dritten Viertel, andere wiederum haben es überhaupt nicht.

b) Fermate etwa 4 Halbe; keine Luftpause danach.

a) Certaines éditions ont le signe: *sf* au troisième temps, d'autres éditions, par contre, ne le donnent pas du tout.

b) Point d'orgue d'une durée de la valeur d'environ quatre blanches. Ne faire suivre d'aucune pause.

a) Some editions have the sign: *sf* on the third beat, others again omit it entirely.

b) Pause about 4 minims. No breathing-pause afterwards.

leggiero
più p
mp
poco
(I.
II.
III.
I.
cresc.
tr
f
VI.)
(𝅗𝅥 = 116)
p dolce
p
mp
mf
leggiero

a) Bei Einigen heißt das fünfte (und neunte) Triolenachtel: „f²“.

a) Dans certaines éditions, la cinquième (et neuvième) valeur des triolets doit être un „fa“.

a) In some editions the fifth (and ninth) triplet quaver is f²

leggiero
molto p
più p
p
pp
p
mp
p
mp
sf
p dolce
p
poco molto
più p
dolce
cresc.
non troppo presto
p, leggierissimo
molto p
poco
più p,
leggierissimo
p
molto p
pp

mp, ma leggiero
poco
p
semplice
p
Ped.
Ped.
p, un poco più sonore
un poco crescendo
non troppo
p
dolce
ca - - lan - -
diminuendo
pp
do
i. t.
molto p
p
leggiero
più p
p
(𝅗𝅥 = 116)
p cresc.
p
cresc.

1) ungestüm / impétueu / impetuously
2) kurz / bref / short

a) Fermate etwa 5 Halbe. Keine Luftpause danach.
b) Fermate beachten!

a) Point d'orgue d'une durée de la valeur d'environ cinq blanches, ne faire suivre d'aucune pause.
b) Tenir compte du point d'orgue.

a) Pause about 5 minims. No breathing-pause.
b) Observe the pause!

SONATE

No. 9

DER BARONIN VON BRAUN GEWIDMET

ALLEGRO (♩= 126) **BEETHOVEN, Op. 14 Nr. 1**

a)

1) *angenehm, wohlgefällig.*
agréable et plaisant
pleasing, agreeable

2) *deutlich*
bien distinct
distinct!

sopra
mp cantando
p
ben legato
p 1) sereno
pp
a)
mp, cantabile
p
dolce
p, semplice
Ped.
sf
f robusto
p 2) gato
pp cresc.
mp
ff
1) heiter
gai
jauntily
2) fröhlich
joyeux
merrily

(Tempo Imo)
pp
p dolce
p dolce
cresc.
fp
p, semplice
ten.
ten.
cresc.
espr. e un poco rubato
f
p
cresc.
trunquillo
i.t.
f
rf
p
dolce

ten.
pp
Ped.
tranquillo
i.t.
p cresc. molto
Ped.
sf
molto p, legg.
p
p
pp
pp
p
p
pp
decresc.
f
Ped.
sf
p distintamente
sopra
Ped.

decresc.
p cresc.
Tempo II.
semplice
mp cantando
ben legato
sopra
dolce

a) v. p. 3a.

a)
mp, cantabile
Tempo I.
un poco cantabile
decresc.
poco calando
cresc.

a) v. p. 4a.

ALLEGRETTO (𝅗𝅥. = 50)
p elegiaco
sf
p
cresc.
sf
p
p
sf
sf
p molto dolce
pp
mp
sf
sf
p dolce
Ped.
Ped.
p
sf
cresc.
sf
sf
sf
mp
p cresc.
p
pp
cresc. poco a poco
mp

sf
mf
f
più f
p
pp
mp
cresc.
Maggiore (𝅗𝅥. = 60)
dolce e cantabile
p cresc.
decresc.
p decresc.
D.c. Allegretto e poi la Coda.
CODA (𝅗𝅥. = 60)
poco cresc.

RONDO

ALLEGRO COMMODO (𝅗𝅥 = 80)

p
decresc.
pp
p
ppp
cresc.
p
sf
più p
sf
p
cresc.
sempre f
sf
sf
sf
sf
sf
sf
crescendo
p
(𝅗𝅥 = 100.)
f
f
Ped.
Ped.

f
p
più p
marc.
(con 8va)
decresc.

pp
più pp
legato
cresc. non troppo
ppp
pp
decresc.
Tempo I.
ppp
p dolce
Ped.
cresc.
p
sf
poco più p
sf

mp
p
cresc.
Ped.
f
p
più p
pp
p
decresc.
cresc.
ff
marc.

sf
Ped.
sf
sf
decresc.
non lunga
p
pp legato, ma leggiero
più pp
pp
più pp
p
commodo
più p
cresc.
f
f
Ped.
Ped.
Ped.
Ped.
Ped.
Ped.

SONATE

No. 10

DER BARONIN VON BRAUN GEWIDMET

ALLEGRO (♩ = 104)

BEETHOVEN, Op. 14 Nr. 2

a) Leichter:
Exécution plus facile:
This way is easier of execution:

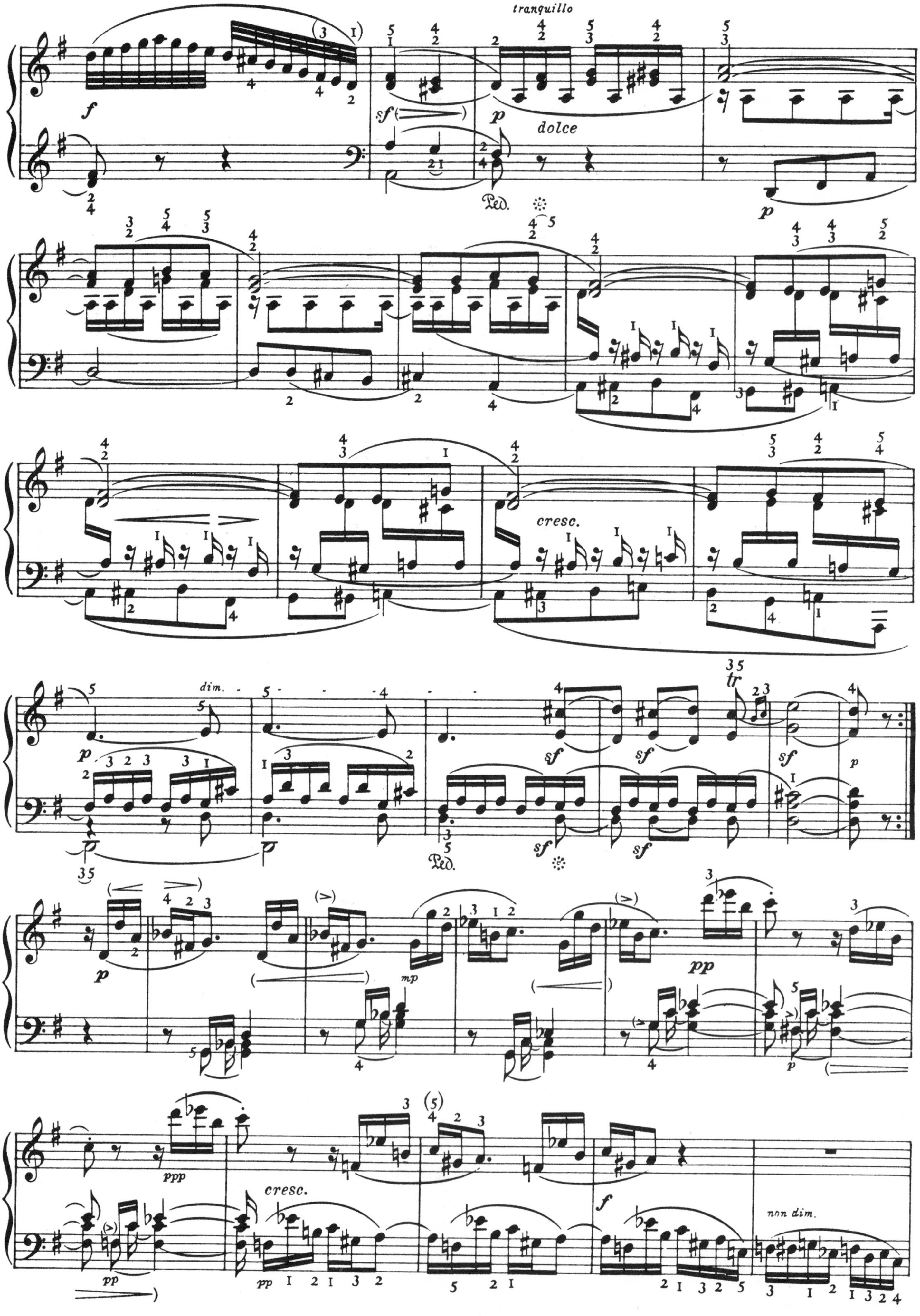

tranquillo

dolce

cresc.

dim.

cresc.

non dim.

decresc.
marc.

sf sf p

mp cresc.

f sf

f sf

f sf

sopra
decresc.
pp
cresc.
f
ff marcatissimo
Ped.
Ped.
non troppo corto
sf
p dolce, semplice
cresc.
sf
p
cresc.
sf

35
pp
cresc.
p
cresc.
leggiero
a)
a) Leichter:
Exécution plus facile:
This way is easier of execution:

p
cresc.
f
sf
Ped.
f
sf
p dolce
Ped.
p
cresc.
decresc.
p
p
cresc.
rf
p
p
cresc.
f
sf
p
più p
tranquillo
p
semplice

ANDANTE (𝅗𝅥 = 72)
La prima parte senza replica
p
cresc.
sf
cresc.
sf
p
p
Ped.
cresc.
p
f
sf
p
sf
sf
sf
sf
p
(𝅗𝅥 = 80)
p
sempre ligato
cresc.
p

cresc.
(♩= 72)
non cresc.
(♩= 80)
1.
2.
(♩= 69)
p dolce
cresc.

p
cresc.
sf
p
f
f
f
decresc.
f
1.
p
p
2.
p
p
mp
decresc.
(♩= 72)
non troppo accentuare
simile
pp
ppp
p semplice
dolce
sempre ligato
p
cresc.
p
rinf.
cresc. molto
mp
rinf.

tranquillo
dolce semplice
p
pp
p
cresc.
f
decresc.
ff

SCHERZO

Allegro assai (♩ = 88)

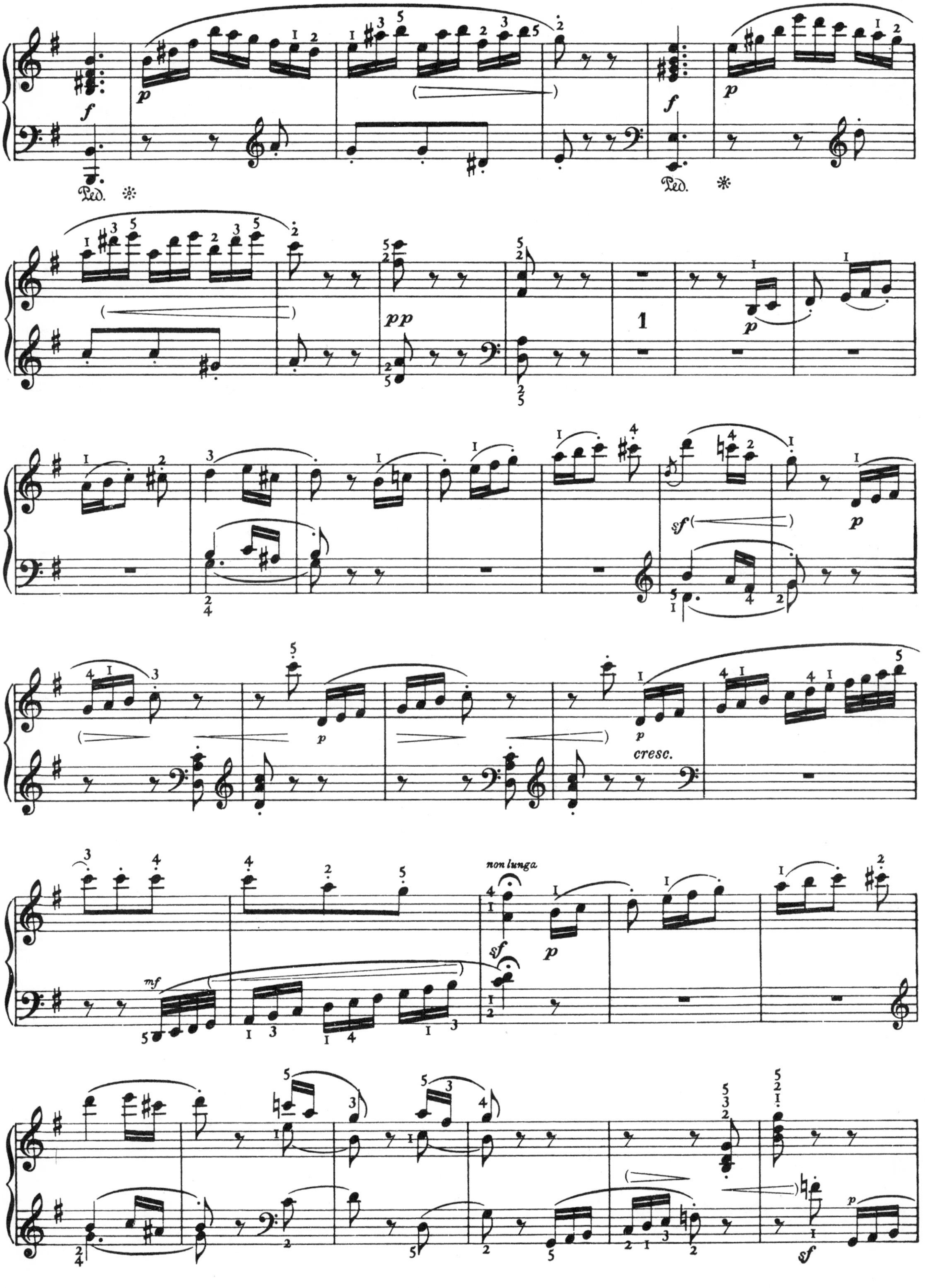

Ped. ※ Ped. ※

1

cresc.

non lunga

crescendo
(♩.= 80)
decresc.
p dolce
molto p
poco

crescendo
decresc.
molto p
poco
(♩. = 84)
decresc.

(♩. = 88)
non troppo lunga
p
più p
sf
p
p cresc.
mf
non lunga
sf
p
cresc.
1

de - cre - scen - do
1
f
pp
poco
non pressare
pp
cresc.
f
p
(♩. = 80)
non legato
p
cresc. poco a poco
sopra
mf sempre cresc.
sf
f cresc.

(♩.= 92)
p leggiero
ff
non legato
sf
cresc. molto,
non accelerare
ff
(♩.= 80)
p semplice
ff
non legato
cresc. poco a poco
pp
Ped.
sopra
mf sempre cresc.
sf
f
cresc.
ff

22 (♩. = 92)
non legato
p leggiero
cresc. molto, non accelerare
(♩. = 80)
ff
ff p
p
non legato
leggierissimo
Ped.
sf
mf
poco
molto
pp
non presto

SONATE

No. 11

DEM GRAFEN VON BROWNE GEWIDMET

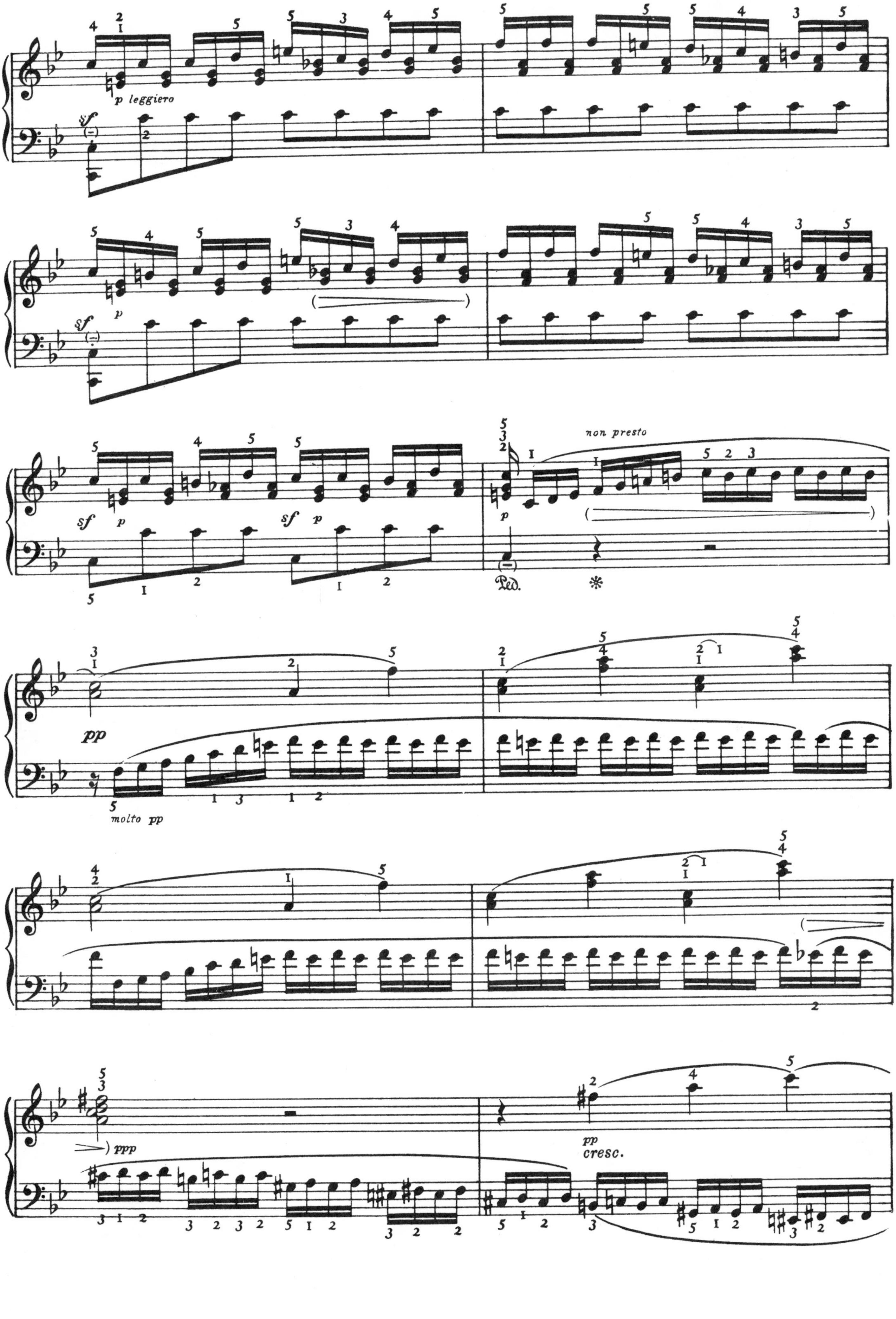

p leggiero

non presto

molto pp

pp
cresc.

pref
sf
cresc.
decresc.
pp
sempre pp
psf
rp oresc.
fz
f
non legato
sfz
sem-

m.s.
ben legato
cresc.
meno legato
non accel.
sempre ritmico
molto
molto p
decresc.
poco

cresc. molto
più p
molto p, ritmico
più p
decresc.
ten.
marcatissimo

(𝅗𝅥 = 176)
mf
molto
p
crescendo poco a poco
f
dim. poco a poco
decresc.
p

pp
un poco meno pp
pp
ppp
pp
cresc.
decresc.
(Tempo Imo)
p
cresc.
pp

a) v. p. 3a

non presto
molto pp
Ped.
cresc.
sempre f
cresc.
f decresc.
sempre pp
cresc.

non legato
ben legato
m.s.
cresc.
meno legato
non accel.
sempre ritmico
molto
molto p
decresc.
poco

ADAGIO CON MOLTA ESPRESSIONE (♪ = 84)
a)
pp quieto
cantabile, ma molto dolce
simile
poco espr.
cresc.
p
più p
pp
sf
poco
pp, ma sonore e con anima
meno pp
cresc.
decresc.
Ped.

a) Der Herausgeber spielt: L'éditeur lui-même joue: The Editor himself plays: [tranqu.] meistens aber ist folgende Ausführung zu hören: en général on entend l'exécution suivante: but generally the following execution is heard:

dramatico
(♪= 100)
cresc.
molto
poco
simile
molto
poco
Ped. simile
cresc.
grave
cresc.
p cresc. poco meno
grave
poco a poco calmando
cresc. non troppo
al

Tempo I
dolcissimo, cantabile
ppp
pp
simile
a)
cresc.
p
poco espr.
cresc.
p
con anima
più p
pp
poco
dolcissimo
poco più sonore
cresc.
sf
decresc.
poco

a) v. p. 13a

ben tranquillo
p, dolce
sf decresc.
pp
m.d.
più p
a)
p, dolcissimo
cresc.
sf
p
cresc.
mf sf
mp sf
cresc.
pp
Ped.

a) v. p. 14a

MENUETTO (♩= 100)

piu p
pp
cre - - scen - do
p
(Più mosso.) (♩= 132)
Minore.
f ma non troppo
legato
sf
f sf piu f
Menuetto D. C.
senza replica

RONDO (♩= 80—84)
ALLEGRETTO
p piacevole
dolce
cresc. non troppo
legato
dolce
legato
cresc.
Ped.
f
[p]
legato
cresc.
p
fsf
p
p cresc.
p cresc.
a) Der Herausgeber spielt:
L'éditeur lui-même joue:
The Editor himself plays:
häufiger empfohlen ist:
en général on recommande de jouer:
more frequently, however, this way is recommended:

(♩ = 88)
f
Ped. ✻
Ped. ✻
sempre f
p
cresc. -
mp
fp
cresc.
pp
f
(Tempo Imo)
fp

non crescendo e non accelerando
poco più p
poco più p
p
p
cresc.
sfp
legato
cresc.
dolce
Ped.

legato
cresc.
f
p
legato
cresc.
p
f
sff
f
f
f
mf
sf
f
non legato
p
leggiero
cresc.

1) *ungestüm*
impétueux
impetuously

(Tempo Imo)
non legato
p leggiero
cresc.
semplice

cresc.

molto p

p dolce e grazioso

poco

cresc.

f

p

un poco rit.

pp

i. t.

p, piacevole, tranqu.

leggierissimo

pp

ppp

a) v. p. 20 a

sempre f
p
cresc.
fp
cresc.
pp
non legato
f
sf
Ped.

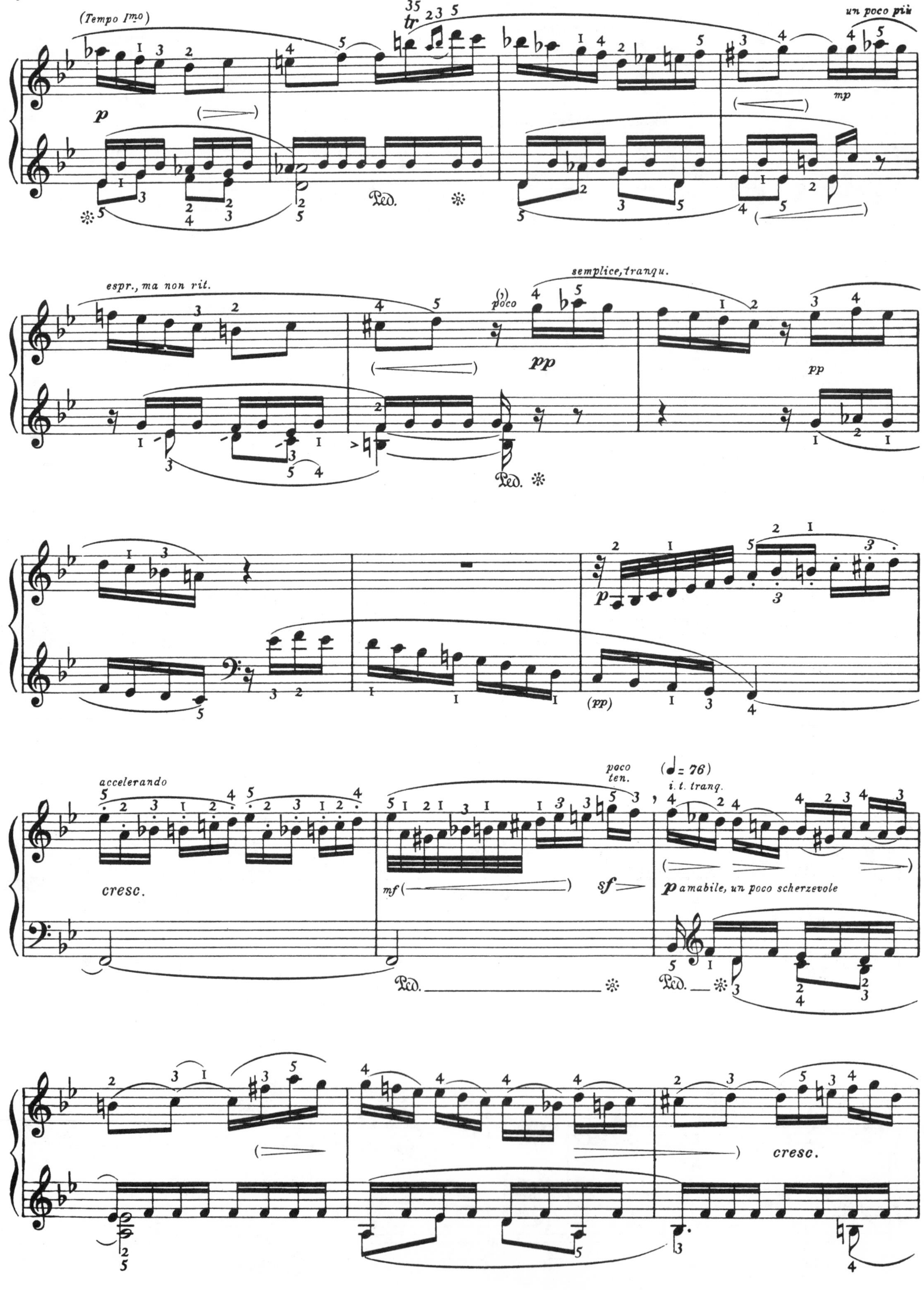
(Tempo Imo)
tr
un poco più
p
mp
Ped.
espr., ma non rit.
poco
semplice, tranqu.
pp
(pp)
accelerando
cresc.
poco ten.
(♩= 76)
i. t. tranq.
mf
sf
p amabile, un poco scherzevole
cresc.

legato
p
cresc.
f
p
(♩= 72)
Ped.
poco
cresc.
f
p
cresc. legato
tr
(♩= 80)
f sf

cresc.
mp
cresc.
tranquillo
più ff
non accel.
sopra
a) Leichter und glänzender:
Plus facile et plus brillant:
Easier and more brillant:

SONATE

No. 12

DEM FÜRSTEN CARL VON LICHNOWSKY GEWIDMET

ANDANTE CON VARIAZIONI (♪ = 63—66) BEETHOVEN, Op. 26

1) edel, ernst, etwas streng.
avec noblesse et gravité, et une certaine sévérité.
noble, grave, somewhat stern

VAR. I

p dolce
Ped.
cresc.
p, ma sonore
non troppo
sf
p
mf ma dolce
molto p
cantabile
mp

ten.
sf
p
p
cresc.
sf
p
mf sf
mf sf
ben articulato
tr
mp sf
p
cresc.
p
cresc.
sf
sf
mf ma dolce
mp
p
p

VAR. II (♪= 88)

1) durchaus ohne Unruhe.
sans la moindre agitation
avoid all restlessness

mp
p
rinf.
cresc.
p
mf sf
p
p tranquillamente
pp
rinf
p
molto p
p dolce
pp

VAR. III

1) tiefernst, gesammelt, gespannt
grave, concentré et tendre
deeply grave, concentrated, intense

2) traurig, schmerzlich klagend
triste, douloureux et plaintif
sad, grieveously moaning

VAR. IV (♪= 84)

a) Das zweite Achtel in der rechten Hand nicht staccato.

a) La seconde croche de la main droite ne doit pas être jouée staccato.

a) The second quaver of the right hand must not be played staccato.

1) sanft und still. doux et tranquille soft and quiet
2) innerlich, mild, liebreich. tendre et affectueux heartfelt, mild, affectionate
3) eindringlich avec ferveur intense

quieto
p dolce
pp
quieto
dolce
pp
sempre dolce e quieto
molto p
poco
più p
poco rit.
cresc.
poco
p dolce cantando
m.s.
cresc.
ma non troppo

a) In der kritisch durchgesehenen Gesamtausgabe steht: mancando, nicht: calando, wie in der Urtextausgabe.

1) aus ganzer Seele, mit aller Hingebung.
**) Pedal autograph.*

a) Dans l'édition complète critique il y a: mancando, et non pas: calando, comme on le lit dans l'édition du texte original.

1) avec beaucoup de sentiment et de ferveur.
**) La pédale est prévue dans le texte autographe.*

a) The complete, critically revised edition says here "mancando," and not "calando," as in the original text edition.

1) with full heart and great devotion
**) the pedal by the composer*

f marc.

f marc.

decresc.

non troppo legato, leggiero e non più presto

poco

non troppo legato

1) ohne Pause weiterspielen
jouer sans interruption
go on without pausing

MARCIA FUNEBRE sulla morte d'un Eroe

Maestoso andante (♩ = 52)

1) *gemessen*
d'un mouvement bien mesuré
measured, deliberate

a) Nicht etwa mehr Zweiunddreißigstel als die vorgeschriebenen: Kein „tremolo“

b) Ped. und ❋ autograph.

1) dumpf, hohl.

a) Jouer exactement le nombre de triples-croches prescrit, et pas davantage: Pas de „tremolo“

b) La pédale ainsi que ❋ sont prévus dans le texte autographe

1) d'un ton creux et caverneux

a) Don't play more than the prescribed number of demi-semi-quavers; no "tremolo"

b) pedal and ❋ by the composer

1) gloomy, hollow

(Tempo Imo)
simile
cresc. non troppo
cresc.
più f
dolce
cresc.
pesante

a) *Ped. und ✻ autograph.*
La pédale ainsi que ✻ sont prévus dans le texte original.
pedal and ✻ by the composer

cresc.
mp
f non legato
f
sfz
p
non legato, leggierissimo
ben legato
molto p
cresc.
f sfz
sfz
6
sfz
sfz
p

cresc.
p
molto p
mp
cresc.
f non legato

non legato, ben articulato
cresc.
non cresc.
ben legato
cresc.
molto p

p
legatissimo
cresc.
mp
f non legato
f
sf

1) verschwinden, verflüchtigen
en s'évaporant, fugitif
vanishing

a) Pedal und ❋ autograph
La pédal ainsi que ❋ sont prévus dans le texte original
pedal and ❋ by the composer

SONATE

Nr. 13.

Sonata quasi una Fantasia

Der Fürstin von Liechtenstein gewidmet

Beethoven, Op. 27. Nr. 1.

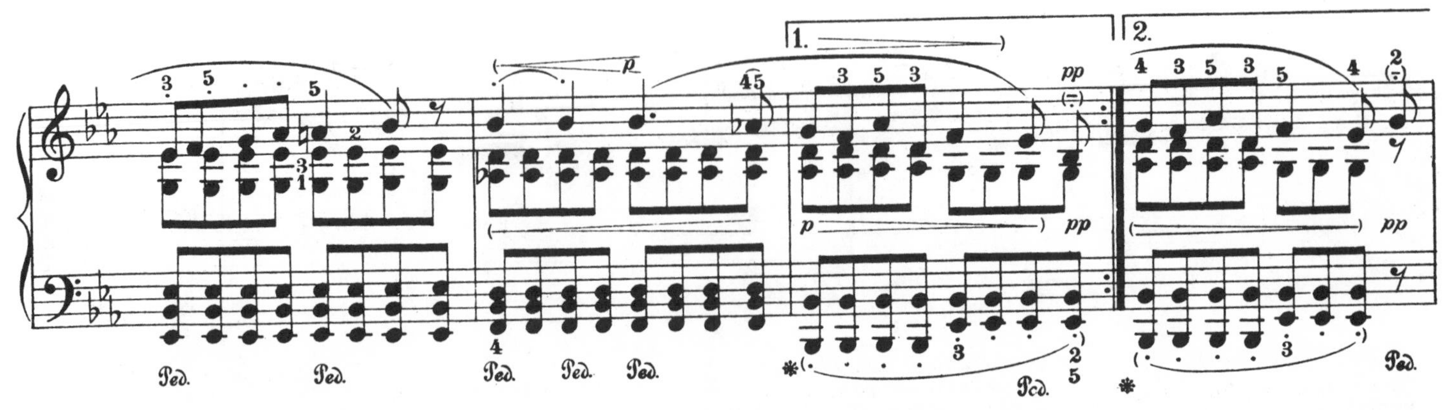

a) Für manche Hände folgende Ausführung vielleicht müheloser:
La version suivante est peut-être mieux à la portée de certaines mains:
This version might be easier of execution for some hands:

b) ungefähr ein Achtel wert.
environ la valeur d'une croche.
About a quaver's worth.

a) Fermate etwa zwei Takte lang: ebenso lang Luftpause danach.

a) Point d'orgue de deux mesures environ, suivi d'une pause respiratoire de même longueur.

a) Fermata about two measures long; the following air-pause the same duration.

Tempo I.

attacca subito l' Allegro.

Allegro molto e vivace. (𝅗𝅥. = 132)

a) *Pedal autograph*
b) *Fermate etwa zwei Takte lang; Allegro unmittelbar anschließen. (Keine Luftpause!)*

a) *Pédale autographe*
b) *Point d'orgue d'environ deux mesures; faites suivre immédiatement l'Allegro (sans pause respiratoire).*

a) *Pedal autograph*
b) *Fermata about two measures long; allegro to follow immediately, without an air-pause*

a) Triller mit der akzentuierten Hauptnote beginnen. | a) Commencez le trille sur la note principale portant l'accent. | a) The trill must begin with the accentuated leading note.

staccatissimo
pp
sempre pp
cresc.
mf
p
Tempo I.
poco
sempre p
non cresc.
f
sempre ligato
distintamente
sempre staccato

a) Fermate etwa acht Takte lang; dann Luftpause etwa zwölf Takte lang. Selbstverständlich darf über eine Luftpause kein Pedal gehalten werden.

a) Point d'orgue d'environ huit mesures, suivi d'une pause respiratoire d'environ douze mesures. Il va sans dire que l'emploi de la pédale se défend pendant les pauses respiratoires.

a) Fermata about eight measures long; then a 12 measures' air-pause. It hardly needs mention that no pedal must be held over an air-pause.

Adagio con espressione. (♪ = 63)

soprano ben cantando, ma dolce

p dolce non cresc.

molto p, egualmente

semplice

cresc.

fp

pp

simile

cresc.

p dolce

molto p

cresc.

rf

decresc.

mf

dolcissimo

pp

intenso, ma non troppo forte

cresc.

più p

ten.

(♪ = 69)

non cresc.

espr. ma non rubato

decresc.

simile

pp poco calando

Tempo I.

dolce cantando

i. t. egualmente

molto p

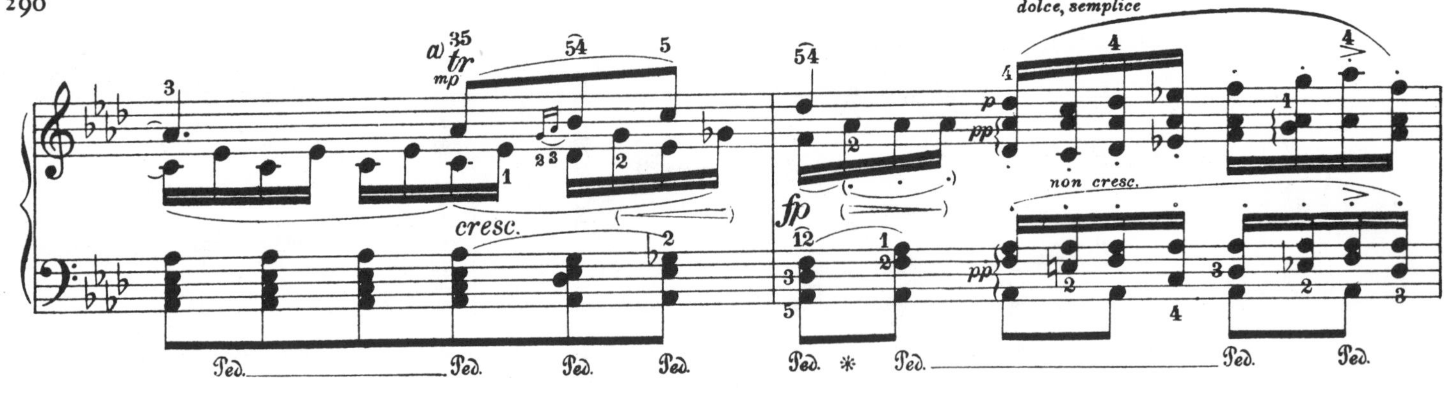

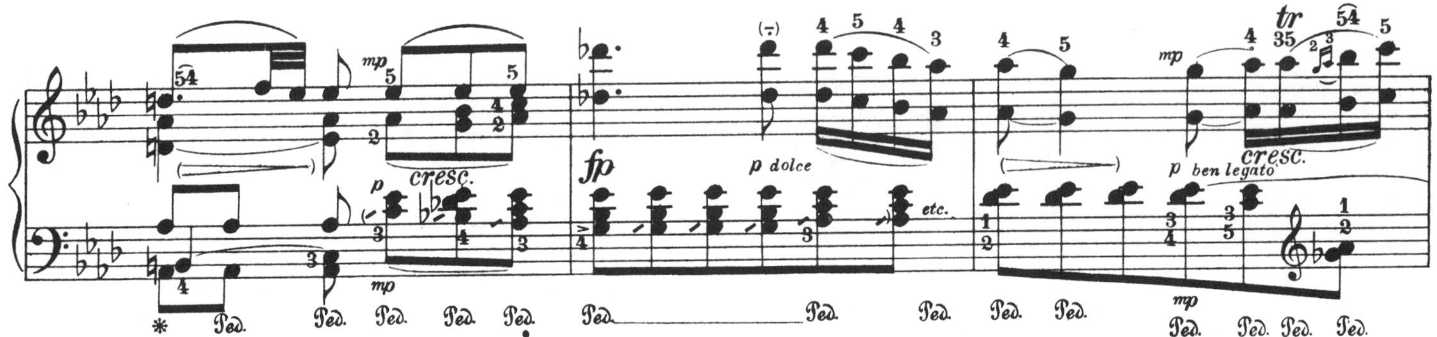

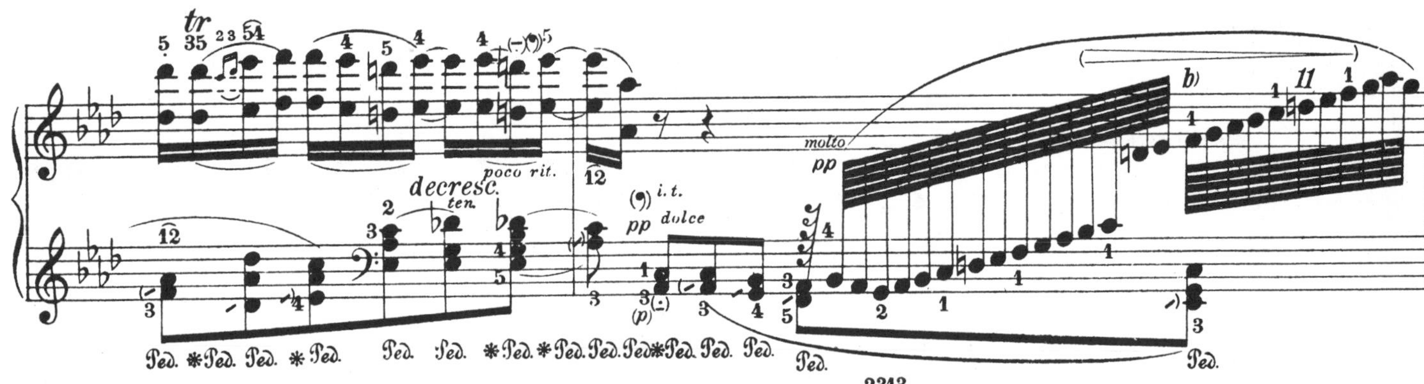

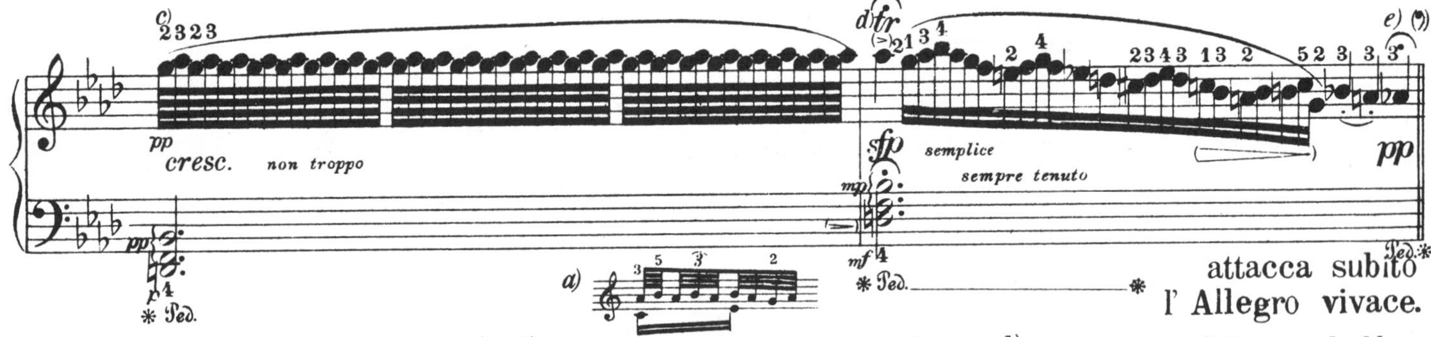

b) Diese Folge von 11 Tönen sollte eigentlich in 64teln aufgeschrieben sein; jedenfalls ist sie um so viel langsamer zu spielen, als die vorangehenden sechzehn 128tel, daß genau der gleiche Achtel-Wert damit ausgefüllt wird.

c) Kein Triller, sondern genau nach der Aufzeichnug.

d) Triller etwa 4 Achtel lang! Mit der Hauptnote beginnen!

b) Cette succession de 11 tons aurait dû être notée en quadruples-croches; en tout cas il s'agit d'en proportionner la durée a celle des seize quintuples-croches qui les précèdent, de telle façon que les deux parties aient la même valeur correspondant à une croche.

c) Pas de trille; conformez-vous exactement au texte.

d) Trille de la longueur de 4 noires environ! Commencez sur la note principale.

b) This succession of 11 tones should properly be written in quadruple quavers; at any rate, it is to be played as much slower as the preceding sixteen octuple quavers, so that the equal quaver's worth is thereby filled up.

c) No trill; play exactly as written.

d) The trill about 4 quavers long! Begin with the leading note!

e) Fermate vier Achtel! Luftpause ebenso lang!

e) Point d'orgue de la durée de quatre croches! Pause respiratoire de même durée!

e) Fermata 4 quavers! The air-pause equally long!

Allegro vivace. (♩= 138)
non legato
cresc.
p ben legato
f non legato
f ben legato
non legato
leggiero
p leggiero
II. etc.
a) leichtere Ausführung:
Plus facile:
Easier of execution:
b) angenehmer:
plus agréable:
More agreeable:

ben ritmico, senza prestezza

p subito

non legato, leggiero

2 sopra

sempre *f*

poco — più *p*

sempre staccato

decresc.

pp tranquillo, ma in tempo

cresc.

p subito — più *p*

pp

cresc.

1) Vigoroso ben legato

sempre *f*

non legato

non legato sempre

(♩ = 144)

sempre *f*

non troppo *f*

mf leggiero

1) kraftvoll, feurig, kernig.
vigoureux
vigorous

a) Die Breitkopf-Ausgaben haben statt f (links zweites 4tel) d; zweifellos ein Stichfehler.

a) Dans les éditions Breitkopf, on trouve ré au lieu de fa (deuxième noire de la gauche); c'est sans doute une erreur typographique.

a) The Breitkopf editions have d instead of f (second crotchet, left) which undoubtedly is an engraver's error.

a) In den Breitkopf-Ausgaben fehlt hier das f-Zeichen; bei Schenker steht es. Kaum ein Zweifel, daß es richtig ist.

a) Le signe f fait défaut dans les éditions Breitkopf; on le trouve chez Schenker. Son exactitude n'est guere douteuse.

a) The f-sign is omitted here in the Breitkopf editions; in Schenker's it stands. It is undoubtedly correct.

a) ohne zu eilen
sans hâte
No haste!

tranquillo, ma in tempo
cresc.
non rit.
Tempo I.
v.p. 12 a)
non legato
ben legato
cresc.
non legato
v.p. 12 a)
legato
leggiero
leggiero
sempre p

v.p. 12 b)
leggiero
leggiero
sempre f
ben ritmico, senza prestezza
non legato, leggiero
subito
sopra
poco
più p
sempre staccato
decresc.
tranquillo, ma in tempo
cresc.
subito
più p
cresc.
basso
sopra

a) *leichter:*
Plus aisé:
Easier:

b) *Fermate etwa 4 Viertel, Luftpause etwa 6 Viertel wert.*
Point d'orgue d'environ 4 noires, pause respiratoire d'environ 6 noires.
Fermata about 4 crotchets worth, air-pause about 6 crotchets.

Tempo I. (♪ = 63)

soprano ben cantando, ma dolce — *semplice* — *p* — *molto p equalmente* — *simile* — *mp* — *cresc.* — *fp* — *non cresc.* — *p dolce* — *pp*

mp — *cresc.* — *p* — *fp* — *p dolce* — *molto p* — *etc.* — *mp* — *cresc.* — *ben legato*

decresc. — *ten. i. t.* — (♪ = 48) — *sfp cresc.* — *p* — *sf* — *p*

a) (♩ = 63) — *p molto dolce e semplice* — *pp* — *poco calando* — (♪ = 63) *attacca* (𝅗𝅥 = 100)

Presto.

p — *distintamente* — *mf sf*

p, non cresc. — *mf sf* — *cresc. sf* — *mp* — *mf* — *f sf*

staccato — *f* — *sempre f* — *sffz* — *più f* — *ff*

Il Fine.

a) *Eine empfehlenswerte Einteilung:*
Subdivision tres recommandable:
A commendable subdivision:

dolcissimo ♩ = 63 — ♪ = ♪ — ♪ = ♪ — *poco calando* ♪ = 63 — *Fermate drei Stel* (♪ = 48)

SONATE

Nr. 14

Sonata quasi una Fantasia

Der Gräfin Julie Guicciardi gewidmet

Adagio sostenuto. (♩ = 63)

Beethoven, Op. 27 Nº 2.

Si deve suonare tutto questo pezzo delicatissimamente e senza sordino.

espr, ma sempre pp e semplice
sost. poco - - i.t.
pp
cresc.
mf, ma dolce
decresc.
p
più
meno
legatissimo dolce
molto p
melodiosamente, semplice

a) Nach des Herausgebers Ansicht dürfen die Viertelnoten nicht hervorgehoben sein; die Triolenbewegung soll in ununterbrochener Führung weiterströmen; bis zur Rückkehr des ersten Themas im Sopran, wo sie wieder Innenstimme ist, immer leiser werdend.

a) A notre avis il ne faut pas faire ressortir les noires; les triolets doivent se déverser d'un mouvement ininterrompu jusqu'au retour du premier thème au soprano; à ce moment, les triolets redeviennent une voix médiale, toujours plus doucement.

a) The Editor is of the opinion that the crotchets must not be accentuated; the movement of the triplets should remain in a continuous current, gradually softening till the return of the first theme in the soprano, when it becomes an inner voice again.

a) Fermate sehr lang, mindestens 2 Takte. Ebenso lang die darauffolgende Luftpause. (Vor dem Allegretto.)

a) Point d'orgue, très long, d'au-moins 2 mesures, suivi d'une pause respiratoire de même durée (avant l'Allegretto.)

a) Fermata very long, at least 2 measures. Equally long the succeeding air-pause (before the entry of the allegretto.)

1) *Einfach, heiter, unschuldsvoll.*
Simple, serein, innocent.
In simple, serene, innocent mood.

2) *Fröhlich.*
Joyeux.
Merrily.

Presto agitato. (𝅗𝅥 = 88)

non legato — *p* — *articolato* — *distintamente, staccatissimo* — *senza* Ped. — *etc.* — *non cresc.* — a) *sf* — *f* *mp* — *senza* Ped. — *sempre staccatissimo* — *sf* — (non legato — *f* — b) — c)

a) Pedal autograph; auch an allen Pararellstellen. *sf* (= *f* Zeichen) gilt nur für das eine (siebente) Achtel; das folgende achte etwa *mp*, und der Beginn des nächsten Taktes wieder *p*. So den ganzen Satz lang.

a) Pédale autographe; de même à tous les endroits parallèles. Le signe *sf* (= *f*) ne concerne que la septième croche; la croche suivante à peu près *mp*, et le début de la mesure suivante de nouveau *p*, et ainsi de suite, tout le morceau.

a) Pedal autograph, also on all parallel passages. *sf* (= *f* sign) only refers to one of the quavers (the seventh one); the subsequent eighth quaver about *mp*, and the beginning of the next measure *p* again. This is to be followed throughout the whole movement.

b) Eine Ausführungsmöglichkeit:
Une manière d'exécuter:
A possible rendering:

c) Fermate nur kurz; etwa fünf Viertel. Keine Luftpause danach.

c) Le point d'orgue doit être court, durée environ 5 noires; pas de pause respiratoire.

c) Fermata but short, abaut 5 crotchets; no air-pause afterwards.

non legato, non cresc.
p
sf
sempre staccatissimo
sf Ped.
p
sf
sf Ped.
p
cresc.
f
non slentare
p subito
molto p
simile
cresc.
p
etc.

a) Von hier ab bis zum nächsten *sf* sind die Bögen vom Herausgeber hinzugesetzt; die Originalausgaben haben gar keine.

a) A partir d'ici jusqu'au *sf* suivant, les arcs ont été ajoutés par l'éditeur; il n'y en a pas dans les éditions originales.

a) From here until the next *sf* the slurs (ties) have been marked by the Editor; in the original editions there are none.

sempre f
Ped.
V.
VI.
I.
II.
III.
IV.
sempre stacc. e p
semplice
non pressare
molto p
cresc.
sempre stacc.
molto p
cresc.
decresc.
p dolce
tranquillo
distintamente
molto p,

a) Nicht etwa die Bewegung unterbrechen zwischen diesem und den folgenden Takt!

a) N'interrompez pas le mouvement entre cette mesure et la mesure suivante!

a) Dont interrupt the flowing motion between this and the subsequent measure!

sf
Ped.
molto
molto p
f
etc.
cresc.
fp
dolce
mp
p

a) Breitkopf sowohl wie Schenker haben hier fis (viertes Viertel rechts); manche Ausgaben hingegen g. Der Herausgeber bekennt sich zu fis.
b) Keine Fermate; keine Luftpause.

a) Breitkopf aussi bien que Schenker ont ici un fa dièze (quatrième noire de la droite); dans certaines éditions par contre, on trouve un sol. L'éditeur a adopté le fa dièze.
b) aucun point d'orgue: aucune pause respiratoire.

a) Both Breitkopf and Schenker have f sharp here (fourth crotchet, right), some other editions g. The Editor thinks f sharp to be correct.
b) No fermata; no air-pause.

a) In der Schenker'schen Ausgabe (Universaledition) fehlt das fp-Zeichen. In den Breitkopf-ausgaben steht es.

a) Dans l'édition de Schenker (Universaledition) le fp fait défaut. On le trouve dans les éditions Breitkopf.

a) In the Schenker Edition (Universal-Edition) the fp sign is omitted; it stands in the Breitkopf editions.

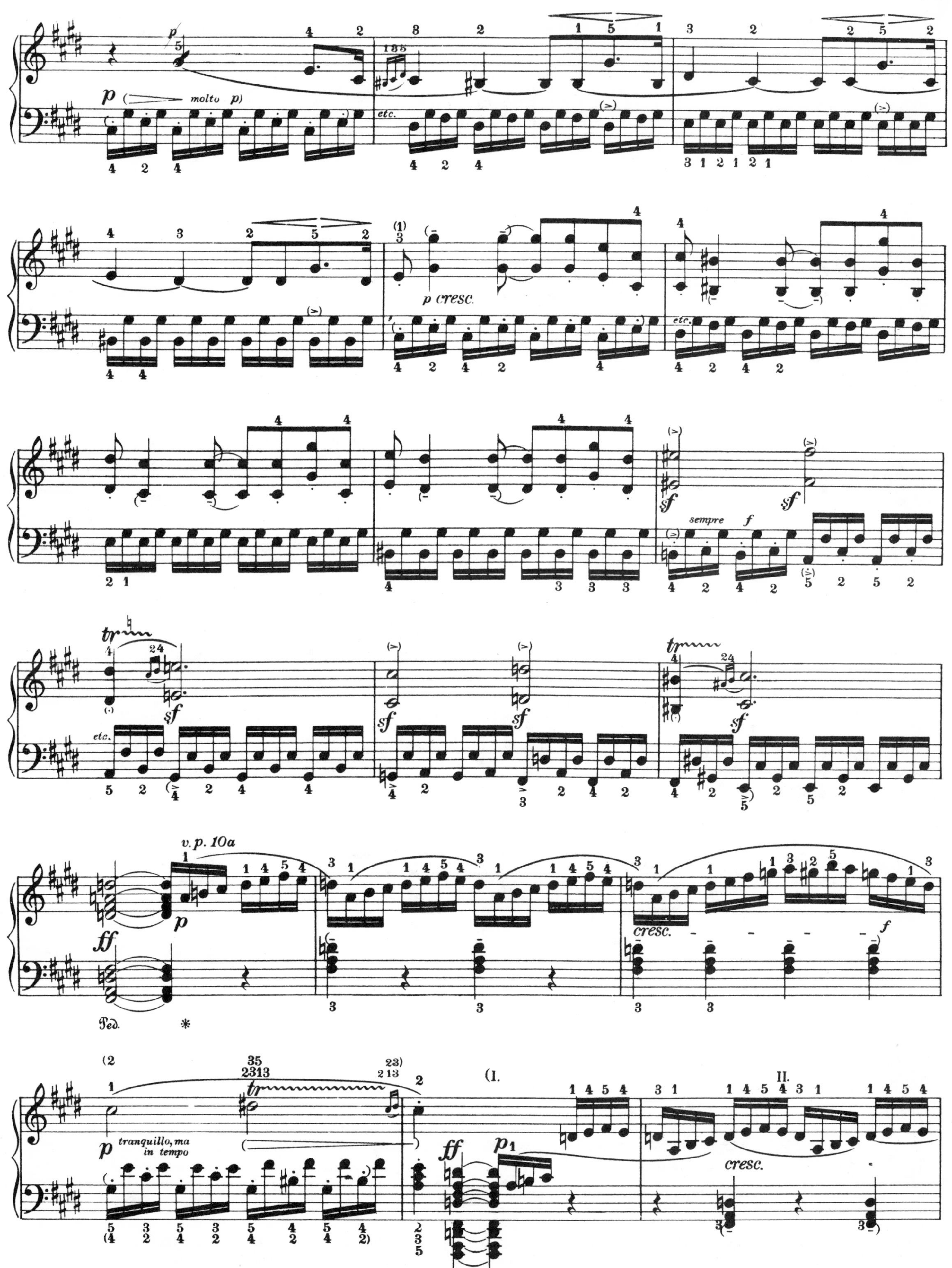
molto p
etc.
p cresc.
sempre f
v. p. 10a
cresc.
tranquillo, ma in tempo
Ped.
(I.
II.

a) Das gis ist nur bei Breitkopf; es ist wohl ein Fehler. Die Terz cis, e- ohne gis dazu- hält der Herausgeber für richtig.

a) Le sol dièze ne se trouve que chez Breitkopf; c'est probablement une faute. Nous tenons pour exacte la tierce ut dièze-mi (sans le sol dièze).

a) The g sharp stands only in the Breitkopf editions; it is presumably an error. The Editor thinks the third c sharp, e, - without g sharp- to be correct.

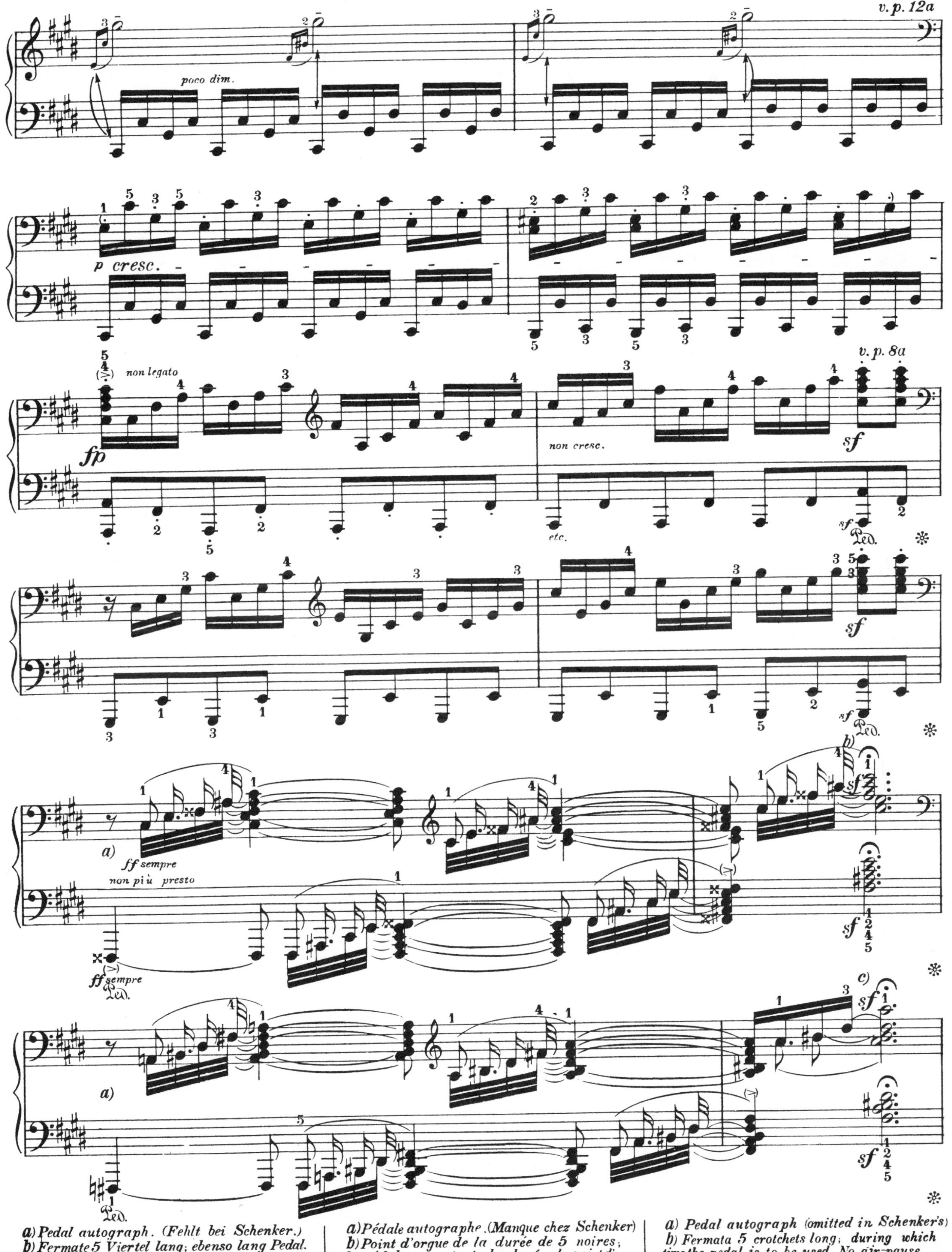

a) Pedal autograph. (Fehlt bei Schenker.)
b) Fermate 5 Viertel lang; ebenso lang Pedal. Keine Luftpause.

c) Fermate 6 Viertel lang; ebenso lang Pedal. Keine Luftpause.

a) Pédale autographe. (Manque chez Schenker)
b) Point d'orgue de la durée de 5 noires; la pédale pour toute la durée du point d'orgue. Pas de pause respiratoire.
c) Point d'orgue de la durée de 6 noires; la pédale pour toute la durée du point d'orgue. Pas de pause respiratoire.

a) Pedal autograph (omitted in Schenker's)
b) Fermata 5 crotchets long; during which time the pedal is to be used. No air=pause.

c) Fermata 6 crotchets long; during which time the pedal is to be used. No air=pause.

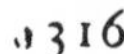

tranq. ma ben in tempo
molto p
etc.
molto p
non legato, leggiero
p cresc.
più f
Ped.

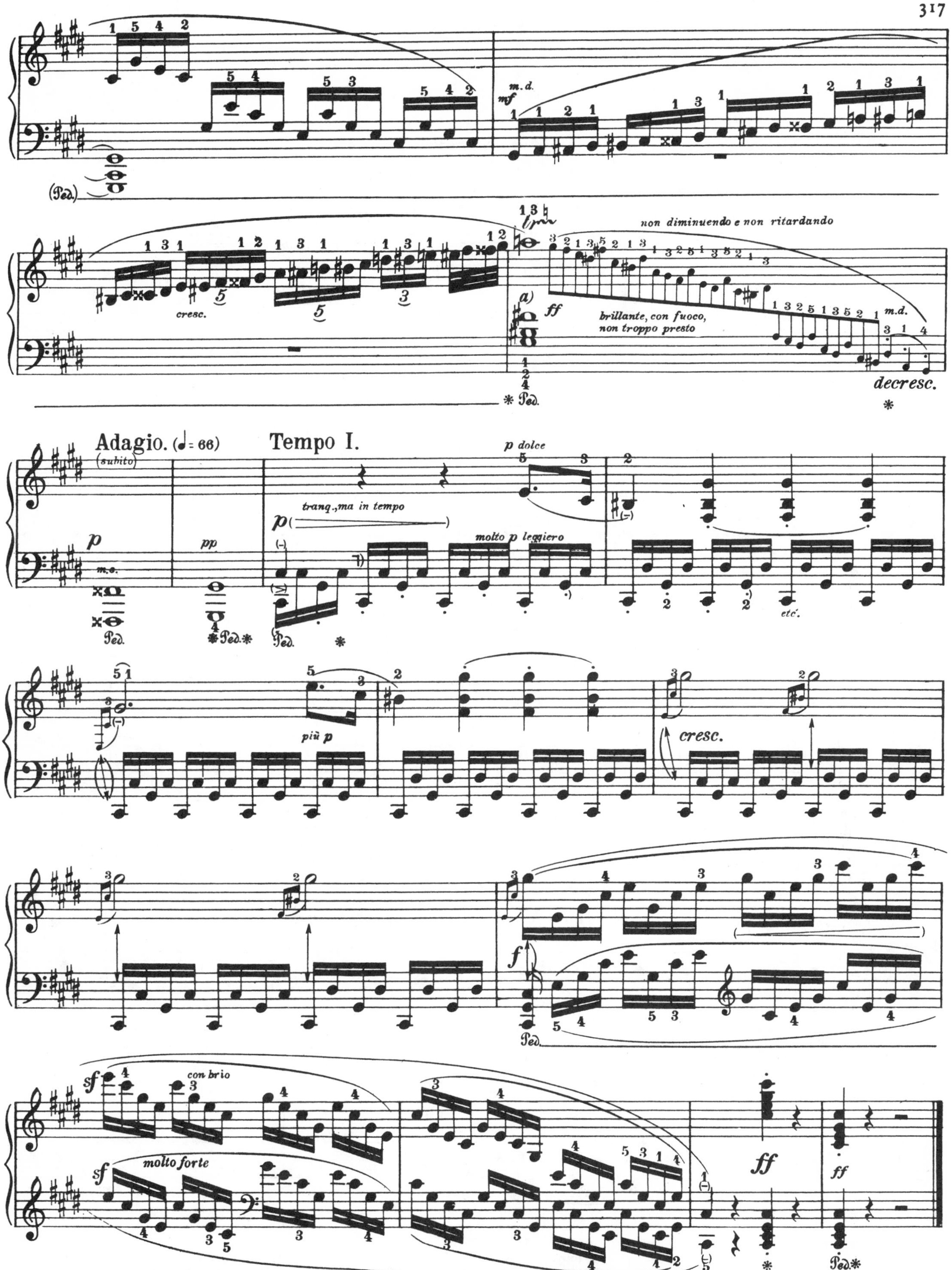

m. d. *mf*

(Ped.)

cresc.

non diminuendo e non ritardando

a) *ff* *brillante, con fuoco, non troppo presto*

m. d.

decresc.

Ped.

Adagio. (♩ = 66) (*subito*)

Tempo I.

p dolce

tranq., ma in tempo

molto p leggiero

m. s.

Ped. Ped. Ped.

etc.

più p

cresc.

Ped.

con brio

molto forte

ff *ff*

Ped.

a) *Eine empfehlenswerte Ausführung (Triller genau 4 Viertel Wert):*

a) *Interpretation fort recommandable (en donnant au trille exactement la valeur de 4 noires):*

a) *A commendable execution (the trill exactly 4 crotchets worth):*

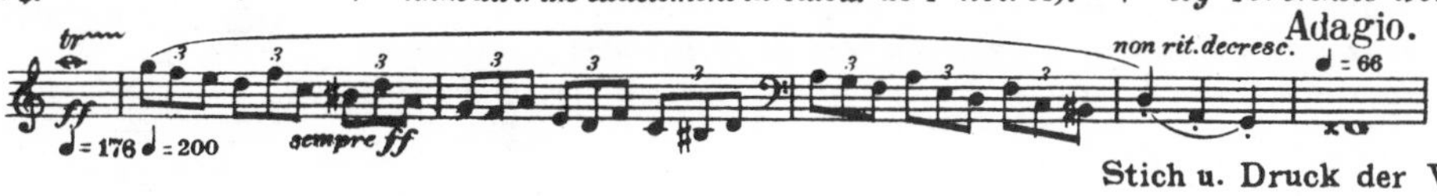

Stich u. Druck der Waldheim = Eberle A. G.

SONATE

Nr. 15

Joseph Edlen von Sonnenfels gewidmet

Beethoven, Op 28.

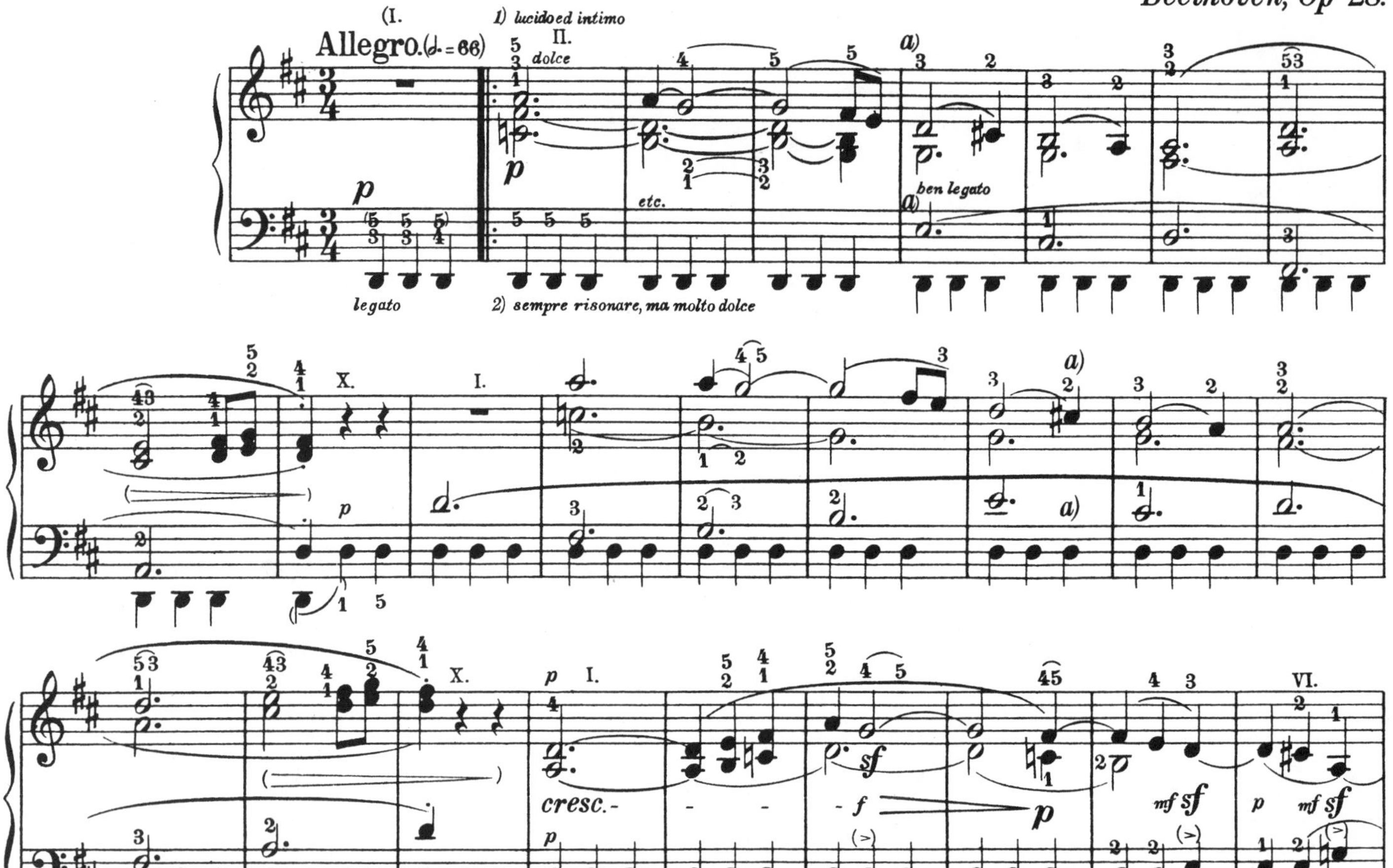

Allegro. (♩. = 66)
1) lucido ed intimo
dolce
legato
2) sempre risonare, ma molto dolce
etc.
ben legato
cresc.
p semplice, non cresc.
p cresc.
IV. etc.)

1) *Klar und innerlich.*
D'une manière claire, venant de l'âme.
Lucid and heartfelt.

2) *Immer klingend, aber sehr weich.*
D'une belle sonorité continue, mais avec beaucoup de douceur.
Always sonorous, but very soft.

a) *Leichtere und wohl sinngemäße Ausführung:*
Interprétation plus aisée et, nous semble-t-il, conforme au sens de ce passage:
An easier rendering which is presumably also in conformity with the meaning of the passage:

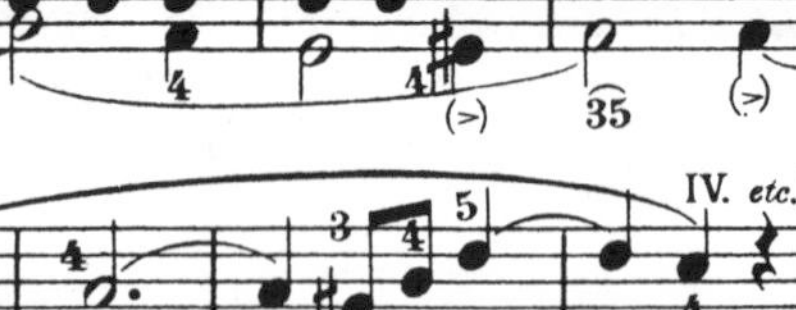

m.s.
etc.

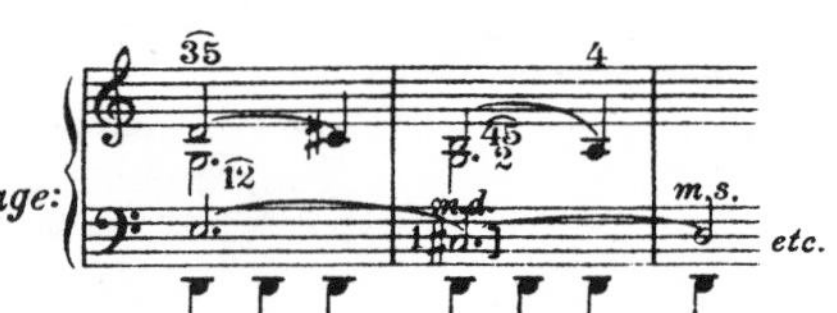

(𝅗𝅥. = 72)
poco
più
cresc.
mf
decresc.
Tempo I
sempre pp
cresc. poco a poco
molto p
egualmente
sempre ben legato
non cresc.
molto p
dim.
quieto
cresc.

a) Die Breitkopf-Ausgaben haben als fünftes 8tel rechte Hand e, Schenker hingegen, der Parallelstelle entsprechend, d. D ist wohl richtig.

a) Les éditions Breitkopf ont un mi à la cinquième croche de la main droite; Schenker, par contre, a un ré, tout comme à l'endroit parallèle; ré semble bien être exact.

a) The Breitkopf editions have e as fifth quaver, right hand; but Schenker puts d, in accordance with the parallel passage; d seems to be correct.

a) Viele Ausgaben haben - im Gegensatz zur Originalausgabe - von d drittes Viertel zu d erstem Viertel einen Haltebogen; das d zweimal anzuschlagen, ist aber vermutlich richtig.

a) Dans nombre d'éditions, on trouve - contrairement à l'édition originale - un arc reliant le ré du troisième temps au ré sur le premier temps; il est probablement plus juste de répéter le ré.

a) Many editions, contrary to the original edition, have a stop = tie from d, third crotchet, to d, first crotchet; but it is presumably correct to strike the d twice.

(v. p. 3a)
p cresc.
mf
p subito
f
p
cresc.
non legato
f sempre
f non legato
sempre p
legato

a) Die Breitkopfausgaben haben hier und im nächsten Takt auf eis im Baß sf-Zeichen; sie sind nicht recht erklärlich, zumal im Takt davor das p plötzlich einsetzt, nach achtmaligem sf im ff. Will man die beiden sf aber ausführen, so muß nach des Herausgebers Ansicht das zweite davon zu fis gehören, und der Stärkegrad der sf selbstverständlich dem p entsprechen.

1) Ohne Wichtigkeit.
2) Führend.

a) Dans les éditions Breitkopf, on trouve ici, ainsiqu' à la mesure suivante, un sf placé à la basse sous le ut dièze; on ne peut guère se les expliquer, d'autant moins qu' à la mesure précédente le p paraît subitement, après la répétition par huit fois du sf en plein ff. Si l'on veut jouer ces deux sf, il faut à notre avis que le deuxième soit placé sous le fa dièze et que l'intensité des sf soit proportionnée, cela va sans dire, au p

1) Sans caractère d'importance
2) D'un mouvement directeur.

a) The Breitkopf editions have here and in the following measure the sf sign upon c sharp in the bass. These signs are not easily to be explained, the less so as, in the preceding measure, the p begins quite suddenly after eight times sf in the ff. If, however, you want to execute the two sf, the second must belong to f sharp, in the Editor's opinion; and the dynamic degree of the two sf must naturally correspond with the p.

1) Without importance.
2) Leading.

a) Pedal autograph.
b) Fermate acht Viertel lang. Keine Luftpause!

c) Fermate vier Viertel lang.
d) Fermate fünf Viertel lang. Auch hier keine Luftpause.
e) Das dritte Viertel dieses Taktes hat ausnahmsweise kein sf; es soll aber wohl mindestens einen Akzent bekommen.

a) Pédale autographe.
b) Point d'orgue de la durée de huit noires. Pas de pause respiratoire!
c) Point d'orgue de la durée de quatre noires.
d) Point d'orgue de la durée de cinq noires. Pas de pause respiratoire, ici non plus.
e) La troisième noire de cette mesure n'a exceptionnellement pas de sf; il faut pourtant, croyons-nous, lui donner pour le moins de l'accent.

a) Pedal autograph.
b) Fermata 8 crotchets long. No air-pause!

c) Fermata 4 crotchets long.
d) Fermata 5 crotchets long. Here, too, no air-pause.

e) The third crotchet of this measure has, exceptionally, no sf; but it should certainly have at least some kind of an accent.

(♩. = 72)

Tempo I.

a) Leichtere Ausführung:
Plus aisé à exécuter:
Easier of execution:

VIII
I
VI
molto p
pp
cresc. poco a poco
mf
equalmente, molto p
non cresc.
sempre ben legato
dim.
quieto
cresc.
non troppo
(♩. = 63)
cantando
mf molto p
Ped.
sf
f

con animu, cantando, ma dolce
legato
molto p
p subito
molto p
legato
Ped.
cresc.
poco a poco
decresc.

a) *Die Fermate wohl beachten!*
Attention au point d'orgue!
Don't overlook the Fermata!

1) Ernst, ein wenig düster, immer gehend. | 1) Grave, un peu sombre; ainsi de suite. | 1) Serious, somewhat gloomy, always a-going.

a) Unmittelbar anschließen; keine Pause zwischen 3. und 4. Achtel!

a) Continuez sans interruption; pas d'arrêt entre la 3e et la 4e croche!

a) Conneot immediately - no pause between 3d and 4th quaver!

a) Einige der Bögen über den 32tel Figuren sind vom Herausgeber hinzugefügt (oder ergänzt).

a) Les arcs au-dessus des triples-croches ont été en partie ajoutés (ou complétés) par l'éditeur.

a) Some of the slurs (ties) over the demi-semi-quavers have been added, or supplemented, by the Editor.

un poco rubato
i.t.
m.d.
m.s.
cresc.
Ped.
molto p
non cresc.
poco
liberamente, molto espressivo
cresc.
sempre stacc.
p, espressivo
legato
un poco rubato
cresc.

tranquillo
sempre p
non cresc
cresc.
marcato
non rit. e non dim.
tranquillo
semplice, serioso
subito
l'istesso tempo
decresc.
sost.
a) Fermate drei Viertel lang; keine Luftpause.
a) Point d'orgue de la durée de trois noires; pas de pause respiratoire.
a) Fermata three crotchets long; no air=pause.
c) Fermate recht lang, vielleicht drei Takte (höchstens).
c) Point d'orgue bien prolongé; trois mesures peut être (c'est le maximum).
c) Fermata rather long; about three measures (ad best).

Scherzo.

Allegro vivace. (𝅗𝅥. = 104)

1) Fröhlich.
a) Fermate zwei Takte. Keine Luftpause.

1) Joyeux.
a) Point d'orgue de deux mesures. Pas de pause respiratoire.

1) Merrily.
a) Fermata two bars. No air-pause.

Trio. (𝅗𝅥. = 92)

p non legato, quasi stacc.

sempre *p*

La seconda parte una volta.

p

ben legato

p

cresc.

p

sf

f

mf

p

Scherzo da capo.

a) Scherzo ohne Pause anschließen.
Faites suivre le scherzo sans interruption.
Scherzo follows without a pause.

Rondo. (♩. = 80)
Allegro, ma non troppo.

a) Eine Entscheidung darüber, ob das 6. Achtel e an das folgende Viertel e stets, gelegentlich, oder niemals angebunden werden soll, ist durch Vergleichung der verschiedenen Ausgaben nicht zu treffen; es herrscht verwirrende Vielfalt, eine weicht von der anderen ab, die Lösungen sind offenbar willkürlich nach dem Geschmack des Herausgebers. Auch dieser Ausgabe bleibt nur ein gleiches Verfahren übrig; auch sie versucht, selbstverständlich, dabei möglichst sinnvoll zu sein. Zwingend erscheint keine der denkbaren Gestalten.

b) Bogen links und rechts vom Herausgeber.

a) La comparaison entre les différentes éditions ne permet pas de dire, si la liaison entre la 6e croche sur mi et la noire suivante sur mi doit se faire toujours, ou seulement par ci par là, ou si elle ne doit jamais se produire; la diversité des versions rend perplexe; l'une diffère toujours de l'autre et les solutions présentées semblent être le produit bien arbitraire du goût personnel des différents éditeurs. Dans cette nouvelle édition, nous nous voyons bien forcés, nous aussi, d'adopter une méthode analogue; nous nous efforçons aussi, cela va de soi, de respecter autant que possible le sens-même de la musique. Aucune des formes possible n'apparaît comme d'une nécessité absolue.

b) Les arcs à la gauche et à la droite sont de l'éditeur.

a) The question whether the 6th quaver e should always, occasionally, or never be fastened to the following crotchet e, cannot be decided by comparing the various editions. You will find there a perplexing variety of opinions; the solutions offered by the Editors are obviously arbitrary, arising from personal tastes and interpretations. This present edition, too, cannot help following the same course; here, too, as a matter of course, the attempt is made to preserve the essence and meaning of the passage. Not one of the possible solutions appears to be absolutely cogent.

b) The slurs (ties) left and right are by the Editor.

a) Der Haltebogen von h 6. Achtel zu h 1. Achtel, der im Breitkopf'schen Urtext fehlt, in den neuesten andern Ausgaben aber steht, scheint hier unabweisbar richtig.	*a) L'arc de liaison qui relie la 6e croche sur mi au mi de la 1re croche manque dans le texte primitif de Breitkopf; on le trouve cependant dans les autres éditions parmi les plus récentes, et nous le croyons irréfutablement juste.*	*a) The stop-tie from b sixth quaver to b first quaver which is omitted in the original text by Breitkopf but is to be found in the latest other editions, appears to be irrefutably correct here.*

a) Schenker hat hier vom Takt vorher einen Haltebogen zu g im Baß. Nach des Herausgebers Ansicht soll aber das g hier noch einmal angeschlagen werden.

b) Fermate sechs Achtel, Luftpause etwa sechs Achtel.

a) Chez Schenker, on trouve ici un arc de liaison reliant la mesure précédente au sol de la basse. A l'avis de l'éditeur, il faut répéter le sol.

b) Point d'orgue de la durée de 6 croches, pause respiratoire d'environ 6 croches.

a) Schenker has here from the preceding measure a stop-tie to g in the bass. The Editor, however, is of opinion that the g should be struck here once more.

b) Fermata six quavers; air-pause about six quavers.

amabile
p
poco
p dolce
(♩.= 88)
molto legato
sempre p
leggiero
p
cresc.
f

(I.
II.
III.)
cantabile, dolce
sf
p
p m.d. dolce
p
poco più p
p, leggiero
m.d.
molto p
p
poco più p
f sf
p
più p
(I.
f sf
p
f sf
p
f sf
p
f sf
f sf
f sf
tr V.)
(♩. = 69)(v. p. 22♭)
f sempre
sf

(I.
V.)
Tempo I.
leggierissimo, tranquillo
sempre molto pp
cresc.
cresc.
poco a poco animando
(♩.=108)
etc.

Più allegro, quasi presto (♩.=120)

a) b) non troppo legato c)

decresc. pp p cresc. poco a poco

f sf sf sf cresc.

ff brillante ff ff

a) Fermate 8 Achtel. Keine Luftpause.
b) Bögen vom Herausgeber.
c) Die Fingersätze über den Sechzehnteln sind von Beethoven.

a) Point d'orgue de 8 croches. Pas de pause respiratoire.
b) Les arcs ont été ajoutés par l'éditeur.
c) Le doigté au-dessus des doubles-croches est de Beethoven.

a) Fermata 8 quavers; no air-pause.
b) The slurs are by the Editor.
c) The fingering over the semiquavers is by Beethoven.

SONATE

Nr. 16

1) Frisch und munter.

a) Das *f*-Zeichen gilt erst bei der Wiederholung des ersten Teiles; das Sechzehntel am Taktende ist beide Male *p*. Der eingeklammerte Fingersatz über g[1] steht auch nur das zweite Mal zur Wahl.

1) Vif et joyeux.

a) Le signe *f* ne se rapporte qu'à la reprise de la première partie; la double-croche à la fin de la mesure doit être jouée les deux fois *p*. Le doigté placé entre parenthèses ne peut être choisi qu'à la reprise.

1) Brisk and lively.

a) The *f* sign is only valid at the repetition of the first part; the semiquaver at the end of the measure is both times *p*. The bracketed fingering over the g[1] can likewise only be applied the second time.

a) *Fermate etwa 2 Takte. Keine Luftpause.*
Point d'orgue d'environ 2 mesures. Pas de pause respiratoire.
Fermata of about 2 measures. No breathing-pause.

1) *Unbeschwert, leichtbeweglich.*
Léger, mobile et joyeux.
Lightly, winged, sprightly.

a) Dieser und die beiden folgenden Takte sind rechts nur mit einer sehr weitspannenden Hand ausführbar; einer nicht ausreichenden seien nachstehende Einteilungen empfohlen:

a) Cette mesure ainsi que les deux suivantes exigent une grande extension, à la droite nous recommandons pour les mains plus petites la répartition suivante.

a) This and the two following measures can only be executed by a right hand with a very wide span. A hand with insufficient span can try one of these divisions:

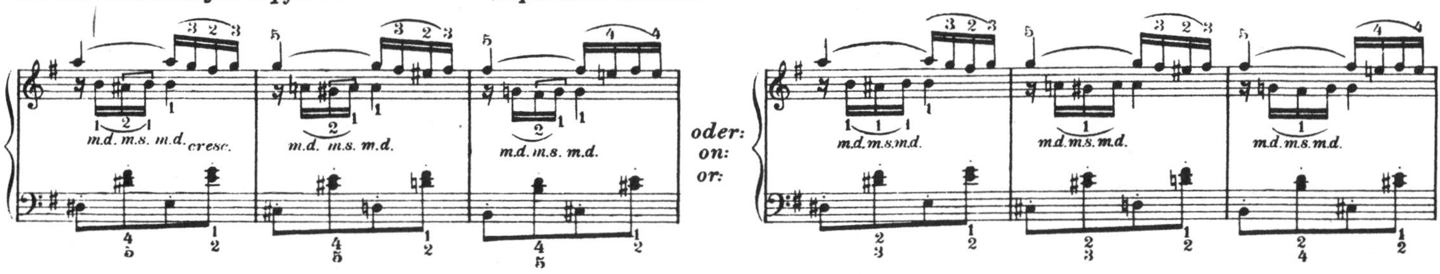

a) In manchen Ausgaben heißt der Baß, hier und in den nächsten drei Takten:

a) Certaines éditions ont ici et aux trois mesures suivantes à la basse:

a) Here and in the following three bars, many editions have the bass thus:

a) *Leichteste (und genügende) Ausführung:*
Exécution la plus facile (parfaitement suffisante):
The easiest (withal sufficient) execution:

sf
sopra
p
f
Tempo Imo

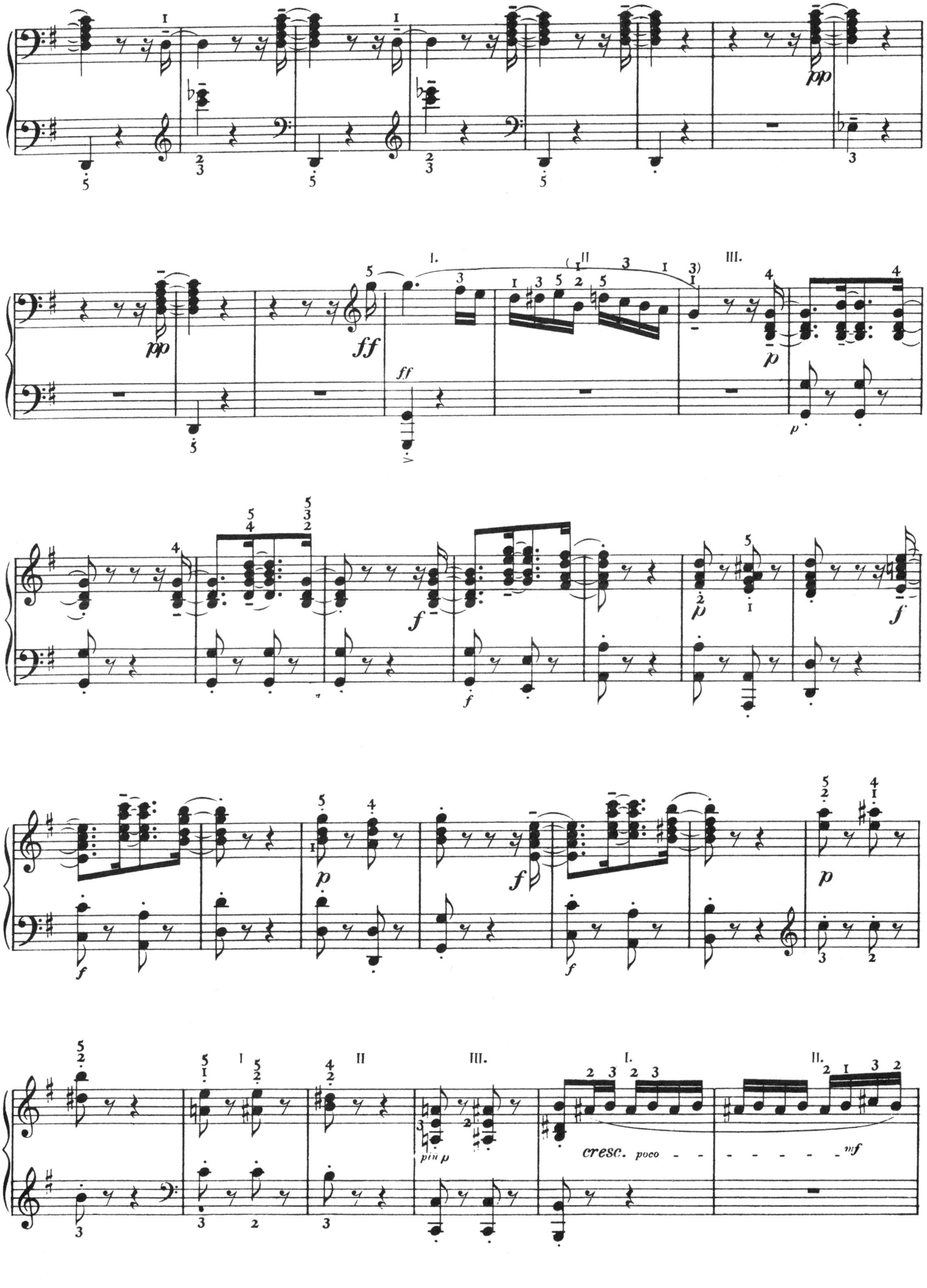
pp
ff
p
f
più p
cresc. poco
mf

(♩= 144) come prima
leggierissimo, molto p
poco
sempre stacc.
mp
molto p
stacc.
f subito
robusto
sf
cresc.
mf
ff
non legato, martellato
delicatamente, mobile
p subito
leggierissimo, molto p
poco
sempre stacc.
mp
molto p

stacc.
f subito
robusto
sf
I.
V.
sempre f
ilare
p leggiero
sempre stacc.
v. p. 6 a)
p cresc.
etc.

p, cantando
marcato
ma non slentare
pp
cresc.
v.p.7a)
ben legato
sempre stacc.
stacc.
Tempo IIdo
ff
non troppo legato
sempre ff

(v.p.4 a)
Tempo I^mo
sf
p
pp
sempre pp
ff

ADAGIO GRAZIOSO (♪ = 112)

a) Dieser Takt kommt (rechts) dreimal in ganz gleicher, ein viertes Mal in rhythmisch reicherer Gestalt vor; nur das erstemal aber ist das sf-Zeichen zum zweiten Achtel gesetzt, sonst steht es immer erst unter dem fünften Achtel (und zwar in allen Ausgaben) und wird überdies durch ein cresc. vorbereitet. Ob die Abweichung bei der ersten Erscheinung des Taktes beabsichtigt ist, läßt sich nicht entscheiden. Aus der Verschiedenheit der Bezeichnung entsteht jedenfalls ein Reiz. Fraglich ist auch, ob das erste Achtel gis zum folgenden jedesmal gebunden werden soll; bei seinem dritten Auftreten hat es nämlich – wiederum in allen Ausgaben – einen Bogen, der die Bindung fordert. Nach des Herausgebers Ansicht ist das legato schöner als die Trennung der beiden Töne, die von vielen Ausgaben durch einen staccato Punkt auf gis (in den drei unbezeichneten Takten) empfohlen wird.

b) Der Fingersatz ist von Beethoven, und zweifellos der denkbar beste.

c) In manchen Ausgaben fehlt das d im Akkord, die alten haben es durchweg.

a) Cette mesure se présente trois fois (à la droite) sous la même forme, et une quatrième fois avec un rhythme plus riche. C'est seulement la première fois, que le signe sf se trouve placé sous la deuxième croche; partout ailleurs, (cela dans toutes les éditions) on le voit sous la cinquième croche de plus il est préparé par un crescendo. On ne peut pas dire, si la différence, que la première mesure présente par rapport aux autres était dans l'intention du compositeur. En tout cas, l'effet produit par cette différence a un charme spécial. Il est sujet à caution si la première croche, sol dièze doit être liée chaque fois à la suivante, car à la troisième apparition de cette mesure, elle porte à nouveau - cela également dans toutes les éditions - une liaison. A l'avis de l'éditeur, le legato est plus beau que la séparation des deux notes recommandée par nombre d'éditions qui agrémentent à cet effet (dans les trois mesures sans indications spéciales) le sol dièze d'un point de staccato.

b) Le doigté est de Beethoven, c'est certainement le plus conforme qu'on sût trouver.

c) Dans certaines éditions, le ré manque à l'accord; il se trouve dans toutes les vieilles éditions.

a) This measure occurs (right hand) three times in perfectly identical, a fourth time in a rhythmically richer shape; only the first time, however, the sf sign is found at the second quaver; otherwise it always stands under the 5th quaver only (in all editions); it is furthermore anticipated by a crescendo. It is hard to decide whether the deviation is intended at the first appearance of the measure. At any rate, a certain charm arises through the variety of the indication. Another open question is whether the first quaver g sharp should be tied every time to the following one; for when it appears for the third time, it has (in all editions) a slur demanding the tie. In the Editor's opinion, the legato is more beautiful than a separation of the two sounds which is recommended in many editions, where even a staccato point is put over g sharp (in the three unmarked measures).

b) The fingering is by Beethoven, it is undoubtedly the best one conceivable.

C) In some editions the d in the chord is missing; it is to be found in all old editions.

a) Der Breitkopf-Urtext, im Gegensatz zu allen anderen Ausgaben, hat den Triller auf dem sechsten Achtel h nicht.
b) Fermate etwa neun Achtel wert.
c) Vier, höchstens aber sechs 32tel auf ein Achtel des Hauptzeitmaßes.

a) De toutes les éditions, le texte primitif de Breitkopf seul n'a pas le trille à la sixième croche sur le si.
b) Point d'orgue d'une valeur d'environ neuf croches.
c) Quatre ou tout au plus six triples-croches pour un temps du mouvement initial.

a) In the original text of the Breitkopf edition, contrary to all other editions, the trill on the sixth quaver b is missing.
b) Fermata about the value of nine quavers.
c) Four-by no means more than six-demisemiquavers to one quaver of the main tempo.

a) Keine Luftpause vor Eins, sondern die Sechzehntelbewegung ununterbrochen fortsetzen.

b) Dieser und die folgenden Takte werden vom Herausgeber in der bezeichneten Verteilung gespielt.

a) Pas de pause respiratoire avant le premier temps; continuez sans interruption le mouvement en doubles-croches.

b) L'éditeur joue cette mesure, ainsi que les suivantes selon la répartition indiquée.

a) No breathing-pause before the first beat; the demisemiquaver movement must be continued without interruption.

b) This and the following measures are played by the Editor in the division designated.

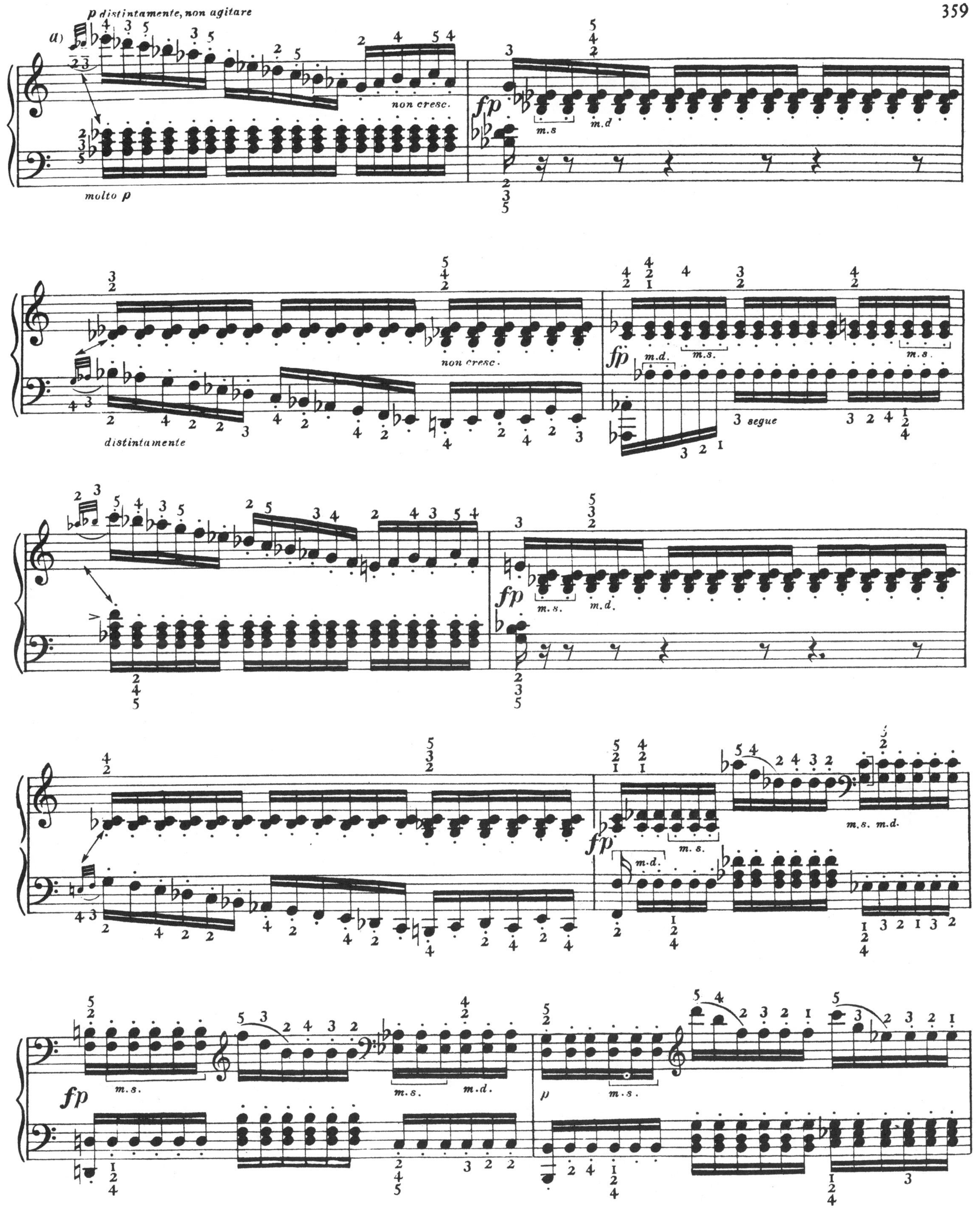

p distintamente, non agitare

a)

molto p

non cresc.

fp

distintamente

non cresc.

fp

3 *segue*

fp

fp

fp

p

a) Der Herausgeber spielt die erste der beiden Vorschlagsnoten genau auf Eins, mit dem ersten Sechszehntel der linken Hand zusammen; betonte Note bleibt aber selbstverständlich das Sechszehntel, zu dem der Vorschlag hinführt.

a) L'éditeur joue la première des deux notes en appogiature exactement sur le premier temps, en même temps que la première double-croche de la gauche; il va sans dire que la double-croche reste la note portant l'accent; c'est à elle que se rapporte l'appogiature.

a) The Editor plays the first of the two appoggiatura-notes strictly on the first beat together with the first semiquaver of the left hand; the semiquaver, however, to which the appoggiatura is leading up, remains of course the note to be accentuated.

a) Luftpause nur kurz, höchstens ein Sechszehntel wert.

a) Arrêt respiratoire d'une durée d'un quart de temps, au plus.

a) Only a short breathing-pause, not more than the value of a semiquaver.

Ped. *

mf liberamente sf
cresc. i. t.
mp mf mp
Ped. * Ped. * Ped. * molto p
p dolce, semplice
leggiero

poco
p
tr
p, dolce, cantando
Ped. * Ped. * Ped.
segue

molto p
leggieramente
(v. p. 15b.)
pp segue
pp p
tr
p
Ped. * Ped. * Ped.

leggieramente
molto p
p pp
Ped. *

sf mf
p dolce
molto p
liberamente, ma sempre dolce
i. t.
più p
tranquillo
pp
cresc.
I.
II.
III.
ben legato

(v.p.16b.)
non troppo presto
(v.p.16c.)
ten.
cresc.
mf poco sost.
p i. t.
dolcissimo, semplice, egualmente
cresc.
f
p
cresc. poco
mf
poco calando
diminuendo
poco, dolce
p i. t.
molto p, egualmente
leggiero
dolcissimo
pp
tranquillo
p liberamente
cresc.
f
ten.
dim.
i. t.
mf
p

a) Nach der Meinung des Herausgebers gilt das *f*-Zeichen von hier bis zu dem decrescendo, das acht Takte später steht; selbstverständlich wird mit dem Stärkegrad auch der Ausdruck dieser Takte wesentlich gesteigert. Die sechs vor dem decrescendo sind nicht mehr im Kreise des lieblich süßen, anmutigen Schwärmens, sondern sie erweitern ihn zu großer erhobener erhabener Empfindung, edler Beseeltheit, beglückter gesammelter Hingabe, zu einem klaren Gebiet, in das weder aufgeregte noch spielerische Töne gehören. Einige Ausgaben haben im Takt nach *f* ein diminuendo, und wiederum einen Takt danach **p**, dann aber bis zum decrescendo gar keine Zeichen, die Stärkegrad angeben. Das decrescendo führt zum **p**; sinngemäß wäre also wohl, daß ihm eine Tonstärke vorausgeht, von der es abnehmend zum **p** gelangt. Der Herausgeber ist von der Unrichtigkeit des **p** vor dem decresc. überzeugt. Die Verlegung des Themas in den tiefen Baß, die Wahl des klangvollsten Klavierteils für die rechte Hand, dazu die *sfz* Zeichen, und schließlich der gedehnte Rückgang-bis zum Ende-fordern hier den Höhepunkt, gleichsam die eindringlichste Verdichtung des Vorausgegangenen; mit leichter und leiser Stimme läßt sich dieser Inhalt keinesfalls erschöpfen.

a) A l'avis de l'éditeur, le signe *f* est valable à partie d'ici jusqu' au decrescendo qui se trouve huit mesures plus loin; en même temps qu'on augmente de force, on doit, cela va sans dire, rendre l'expression d'autant plus intensive. Les six mesures qui précèdent le decrescendo ne se meuvent plus dans la région des douces, tendres et gracieuses rêveries; elles élargissent l'horizon pour atteindre la grandeur, le sublime, la noblesse du sentiment, le bonheur d'un dévouement recueilli, une région pleine de clarté, où n'ont pas de place les tons agités ou enjoués. – Dans plusieurs éditions, on trouve un diminuendo dans la mesure qui suit le *f*; une mesure plus loin: **p**, et ensuite, pas de signes dynamiques jusqu' au decrescendo. Or le decrescendo amène le **p**; il serait donc logique de le faire précéder d'un degré dynamique plus fort, à partir duquel le ton diminuerait jusqu' au **p**. Nous sommes convaincus que le **p** placé devant le decrescendo est faux. Le thème a passé dans les profondeurs de la basse; pour la main droite a été choisie la partie la plus sonore du clavier; à quoi viennent s'ajouter les *sf*, et finalement le retour très extensif jusqu'à la conclusion: tout cela fait de ce passage le point culminant, la contraction la plus intensive, pour ainsi dire, de tout ce qui précède; ce n'est pas avec une expression naïve et douce qu'on arrivera à rendre justice à ce contenu.

a) In the Editor's opinion, the *f* sign is valid from here to the decrescendo which begins eight bars later; as a matter of course, the expression of these measures is essentially heightened corresponding to their dynamic degrees. The six measures before the decrescendo are lifted from the realm of lovely, sweet and graceful revelling; they are expanding it to grand, uplifted sentiments, noble animation, blissful, concentrated devotion – a domain unfit for excited or playful sounds. Some editions have a diminuendo in the measure after *f*, and one measure afterwards a **p**, but then until the decrescendo no sign whatever indicating a dynamic degree. The decrescendo leads straightway to the **p**; it would therefore be logical to have it preceded by a dynamic nuance from which it may properly glide down to the **p**. The Editor is convinced that the **p** before the decrescendo is incorrect. The shifting of the theme to the deep bass; the selection of the best-sounding part of the instrument for the right hand; moreover the *sfz* signs; and, finally, the distended retrogression – distended until the end – all this calls for a climax, the most intense condensation, as it were, of all that has preceded. The contents and essence of all this can by no means be fully expressed simply by a soft and easy voice

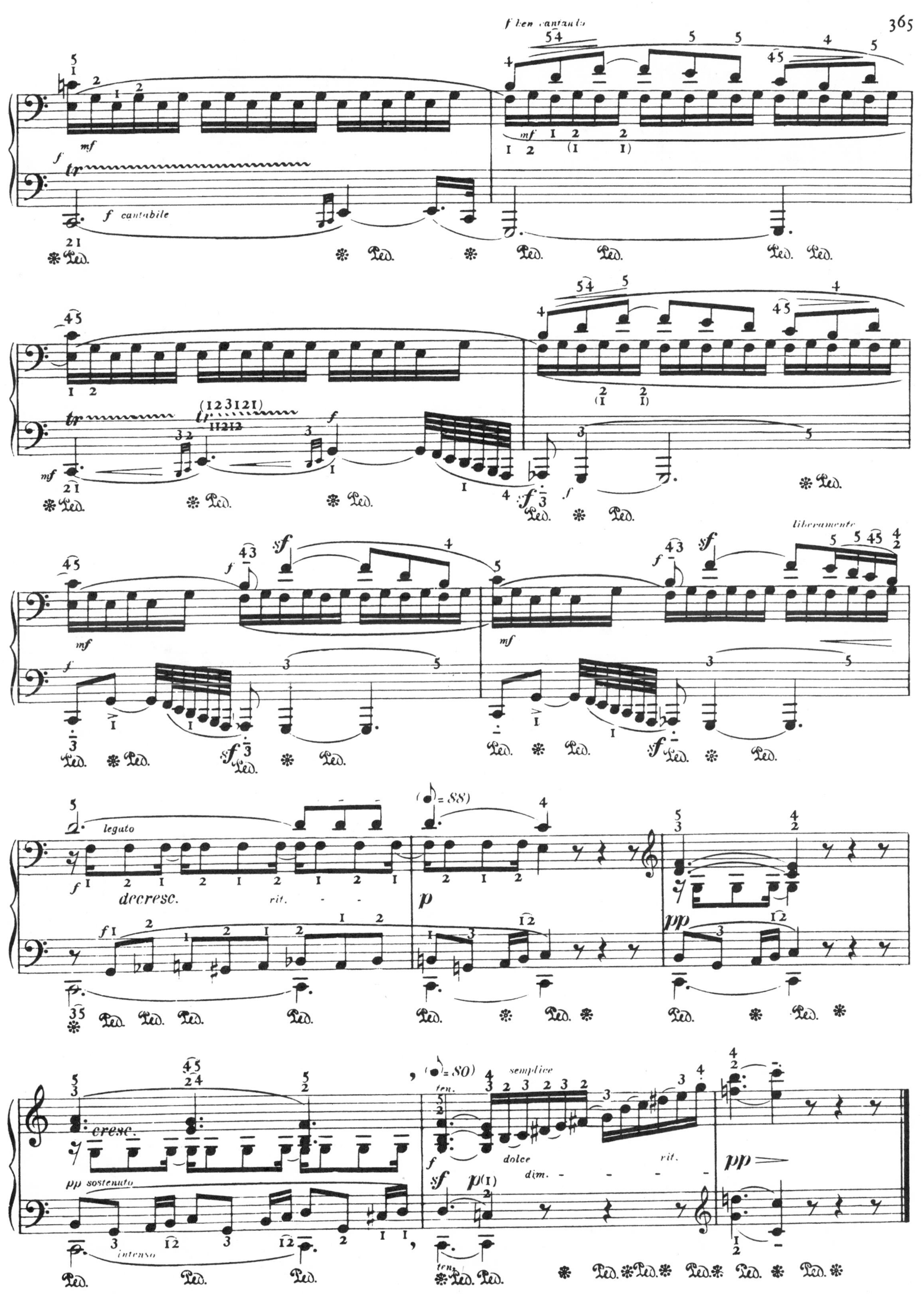
f ben cantando
f cantabile
liberamente
leguto
decresc.
rit.
(♪. = 88)
cresc.
pp sostenuto
intenso
(♪. = 80)
semplice
ten.
dolce
dim.

RONDO

1) In guter, fröhlicher Laune, ganz sorglos, doch etwas eigensinnig.
2) Ohne Eile.
a) In manchen Ausgaben g statt h; h ist zweifellos richtig.

1) De bonne humeur, gaîment, libéré de tout souci, mais un peu capricieux.
2) Sans hâte.
a) Dans certaines éditions, on trouve sol au lieu de si; si est certainement juste.

1) In good, merry humour, entirely free from care, although a little capricious.
2) Without haste.
a) Some editions have a g instead of b; b is undoubtedly correct.

a) Nach des Herausgebers Ansicht p schon auf das erste Achtel. (An der Parallelstelle fehlt es überhaupt.)

a) A l'avis de l'éditeur, le p doit déjà commencer à la première croche. (Il fait totalement défaut au passage correspondant.

a) In the Editor's opinion p must begin already at the first quaver. (At the corresponding passage it is missing altogether).

a) Der Herausgeber spielt diesen - und alle ähnlichen Takte - rechts zweiteilig. also 6 Werte = 2 Vierteltriolen auf 4 Viertel links, etwa:

a) L'éditeur répartit cette mesure et toutes les mesures similaires à la droite en deux groupes de 6 valeurs 2 triolets de croches pour quatre valeurs de noires à la gauche:

a) The Editor plays this measure, as well as all similar ones, in twos in the right hand; therefore 6 values, i. e. 2 crotchet-triplets to 4 crotchets, left; something like this:

II.
III.
amabile
fp più p
pp
p
mp
non legato, sempre leggierissimo
molto p
poco
cresc.
ben legato
f
p
mp
cresc.
f
p
p
molto p, leggiero

(𝅗𝅥 = 104)
più p, deciso
cresc.
m.s.
(𝅗𝅥 = 108)
un poco string.
cresc.
ff
molto
crescendo
poco più p
crescendo
p dolce
poco più p

I.
II.
non cresc.
f subito
sempre f
sf
III.
sempre f
energico
non legato
cresc.
decresc.
p
fp
mf
più p
fp v. p. 27 a)
leggiero
(𝅗𝅥 = 104)
dim.
(𝅗𝅥 = 100)

a) Immer weiter zweiteilig (2×3).
Continuez la répartition en deux (2×3).
Continually in twos (2×3).

v.p. 27a)
cresc.
mp
f
p
cresc.
leggierissimo
f
leggierissimo
p
p dolce
molto p
mp poco cresc.
mf poco dim.

(𝅗𝅥 = 108)
p cresc.
mf
sff
p cresc.
sf mp cresc.
sf
sff
Tempo Imo
sf p
leggiero
melodiosamente
cresc.
p
f
sf
mp
cresc.

a) In einigen alten Ausgaben fängt die Bewegung der gebrochenen Oktaven auf dem zweiten Viertel mit dem unteren g an; wahrscheinlich ein Stichfehler.

a) Dans plusieurs vieilles éditions, le mouvement des octaves brisées commence au deuxième temps sur le sol inférieur; c'est probablement une faute de gravure.

a) In some old editions the movement of the broken octaves begins at the second beat with the lower g, which is probably an engraver's error.

a) Fermate zwei Halbe. Ohne Luftpause weiter.

a) Point d'orgue de la durée de deux blanches. Continuez sans pause respiratoire.

a) Fermata two minims long. Go on without a breathing-pause.

a) Manche Ausgaben haben auch hier und in den beiden folgenden Takten staccato-Punkte; der Herausgeber hält sie für falsch und unangebracht. Aber verlängert dürfen die Viertel selbstverständlich auch nicht sein.

b) Fermate beachten!

a) Certaines éditions ont également ici et aux deux mesures suivantes des points de staccato; l'éditeur les considère comme faux et déplacés. Toutefois il va de soi que les noires ne doivent pas être tenues au-delà de leur valeur.

b) Observez le point d'orgue!

a) Some editions have staccato dots here, too, as well as in the two following measures; the Editor believes them to be erroneous and out of place. But, on the other hand, the crotchets are only to be given their exact value.

b) Do not overlook the fermata!

SONATE
Nr. 17

BEETHOVEN, Op. 31 Nr. 2

a) Der 4 Viertel Takt der kritischen Gesamtausgabe (Br. u. H.) ist zweifellos falsch.

b) Pedal autograph.

c) Fermate etwa fünf 4 tel wert. Keine Luftpause danach.

a) La mesure à 4 temps, telle qu'on la trouve dans l'édition critique générale (Br. et. H.) est, sans nul doute, erronée.

b) Pédale autographique.

c) Point d'orgue d'une durée d'environ 5 temps continuez sans faire de pause.

a) The time-signature C (4/4) of the complete critical edition (Br. & H.) is undoubtedly erroneous.

b) Pedal autograph.

c) Fermata about the value of 5 crotchets; continue without breathing pause.

d) 

e) Fermate etwa 3 Viertel.
Point d'orgue d'une durée d'environ 3 temps.
Fermata about 3 crotchets.

a) Der Herausgeber schlagt vor, die Takte von hierab rhythmisch wie folgt einzuteilen:

a) A partir d'ici, l'éditeur propose la repartition rythmique suivante de ce mouvement.

a) From here onwards the Editor suggests dividing the measures rhythmically as follows:

also 4tel Triole auf den Halbtakt.

c'est-a-dire un triolet de noires pour chaque demi-mesure.

i.e., a-triplet crotchet on the half-beat.

crescendo
sopra
sempre ff
sempre legato
poco
cresc.

III.
I.
II.
III.)
sempre f
f decresc.
(I.
sempre p
poco
più
VI.
I
non cresc.
cresc.
VI.)
p subito

a) Pedal autograph.

b) Fermate etwa 5 Viertel. Pause danach genau.

c) Fermate etwa 6 Viertel. Keine Pause danach.

a) Pédale autographique.

b) Point d'orgue d'une durée d'environ 5 temps; observer strictement la durée de la pause suivante.

c) Point d'orgue d'une durée d'environ 6 temps continuez sans faire de pause.

a) Pedal autograph.

b) Fermata about 5 crotchets; the pause following to be strictly observed.

c) Fermata about 6 crotchets; no pause afterwards.

ALLEGRO
(v. p. 4 (a))
ff
p
sopra
Ped.
f(f)
sempre f
[f]
sf

a) Die großen Bögen-über den kleinen originalen-sind vom Herausgeber.

a) Les grandes liaisons au-dessus des petites liaisons de l'original sont de l'éditeur.

a) The large ties (above of the smaller ones, which are original) are the Editor's.

a) In diesem Takt hat die kritische Gesamtausgabe (Br. u. H.) ein rallent.; in der Urtextausgabe fehlt es. Der Herausgeber hält das rallent. keinesfalls für einen Verstoß gegen den Geist dieses Stückes; wer es fühlt, mag es getrost ausführen, wer es nicht fühlt, unterlassen.
b) Pedal autograph; muß (furchtlos) befolgt werden. Pedalwechsel bringt diese Takte um ihren tiefen Hintergrund, um ihr inneres Wesen.

c) Keine Fermate!
d) Fermate etwa zwei Viertel.

e) Fermate etwa sechs Viertel; keine Luftpause danach.
f) Manche Ausgaben haben hier-letztes Sechzehntel-c statt des; der Herausgeber glaubt unbedingt an des.

a) A cette mesure, l'édition critique générale (Br. et H.) note un rallent.; qui manque dans l'édition du texte original. A l'avis de l'éditeur, ce rallent, n'est d'aucune façon contraire au caractère du morceau; il est laissé libre gré à chacun d'exécuter ce passage selon sa propre conception.
b) Pédale autographique qui doit (strictement) être observée. Toute modification de celle-ci enlèverait à ces mesures de leur caractère profond et de le leur valeur essentielle.
c) Pas de point d'orgue!
d) Points d'orgue d'une durée d'environ deux temps.
e) Point d'orgue d'une durée d'environ six temps continuez sans faire de pause.
f) Dans plusieurs éditions, la dernière double croche est un ut au-lieu d'un ré bémol l'éditeur est convaincu de la justesse du ré bémol.

a) The complete critical edition (Br. e H.) has a rallentando here which is missing in the original text edition. The Editor does not in any way consider this rall, to be an offence against the spirit and essence of this piece. Whoever "feels" it, may execute it unhesitatingly; who does not, may leave it alone.
b) Pedal autograph; must be used fearlessly; A change of pedal would deprive these measures of their deep background, their innermost spirit.
c) No fermata!
d) Fermata about two crotchets.

e) Fermata about six crotchets, no breathing pause afterwards.
f) Some editions have here (last semiquaver) c instead of d ♭ the Editor firmly believes d ♭ to be correct.

a) Die kritische Gesamtausgabe (Br. u. H.) hat hier, zu erstem Viertel, *ff*; es ist vermutlich richtig, jedenfalls aber überzeugend.

a) L'édition critique générale (Br. et H.) note au premier temps un *ff*; c'est probablement exact et, en tout cas, très convaincant.

a) The complete critical edition (Br. e. H.) has here (first crotchet) *ff*; this is presumably correct; at any rate it is convincing.

II.
III.)
sempre f
f dim.
(I.
sempre p
poco
più
VI.
non cresc.
(I)
cresc.
VI.)
p subito

a) Pedal autograph.

b) Die kritische Gesamtausgabe hat hier: das ist wahrscheinlich falsch.

c) Fermate etwa drei Halbe.

a) La pédale est autographique.

b) Dans l'édition critique générale on trouve ici: ce qui est probablement faux.

c) Point d'orgue d'une durée d'environ trois blanches.

a) Pedal autograph.

b) The complete critical edition has here: which is very likely wrong.

c) Fermata about three minims.

ADAGIO
(♩= 44)
dolce cantando
semplice sonore
dolce
ten.
non troppo presto
leggieramente dolcissimo
cresc.
dolce
ten.
non dim.
(♩= 48)
non troppo presto e non troppo secco
distintamente, un poco marc.
soprano ben cantando, con solemnità
cresc.
non slentare,
sopra
oder:
ou bien:
or:
Die Ausführung:
mag der Herausgeber nicht; sie fälscht die rhythmische Gestalt.
La version suivante:
ne nous plaît pas; elle fausse la disposition rythmique.
This way of executing:
is not to the Editor's liking; it falsifies the rhythmic form.

fluente, con passione
cresc.
sost.
f
(f)
(♩=44)
p
dolce subito
poco
più p
tranq. dim. - - molto
pp
ppp
(♩=48)
p dolce, molto semplice, consolante
non presto
mp
poco sost.
cresc.
ten.
sempre pp
non presto
cresc.
pp
cresc.
p
pp
cresc. -

(♩=44)
mf
sf
decresc.
non rit.
molto
p
dolce
v. p. 14b
sempre dolce
mp
sf
p
cresc.
tranqu.
dolce
dolce, cantabile
sopra
molto p, senza fretezza,
egualmente, tranquillo fluente

ten.
poco
non dim.
un poco marc.
soprano ben cantando, con solemnità
cresc.
non slentare, fluente, con passione
sopra

sost.
(♩=44)
dolce
subito
poco
più p
decresc.
molto
tranqu.
non presto
poco sost.
cresc.
(♩=48)
p, dolce
sempre pp
cresc.
cresc.
cantando
cresc.

b) Der Herausgeber zieht hier den nachschlaglosen Triller vor.
L'éditeur préfère ici le trille sans note complémentaire.
Here the Editor prefers the trill without the turn.

ALLEGRETTO (♩.=69)
p semplice
poco
sempre legato
(♩.-76)
agitato, ma non pressare
cresc.
dim.
p
cresc.
f
non string.
p subito
cresc.
dim.
p
cresc.
f
sf espr.
f

cresc.
più espr.
VI) (♩. = 84)
cresc.
con fuoco
ben marc.
non legato
marc.
sempre f
passionato
non legato, sempre
dim.
Ped.
a)

v.p. 21 a

p semplice

non legato

f

sf *dim.*

mp

p

sempre non legato

un poco stringendo

p *cresc.*

f

(♩. = 76) (I. tranqu., ma in tempo

p subito

non legato

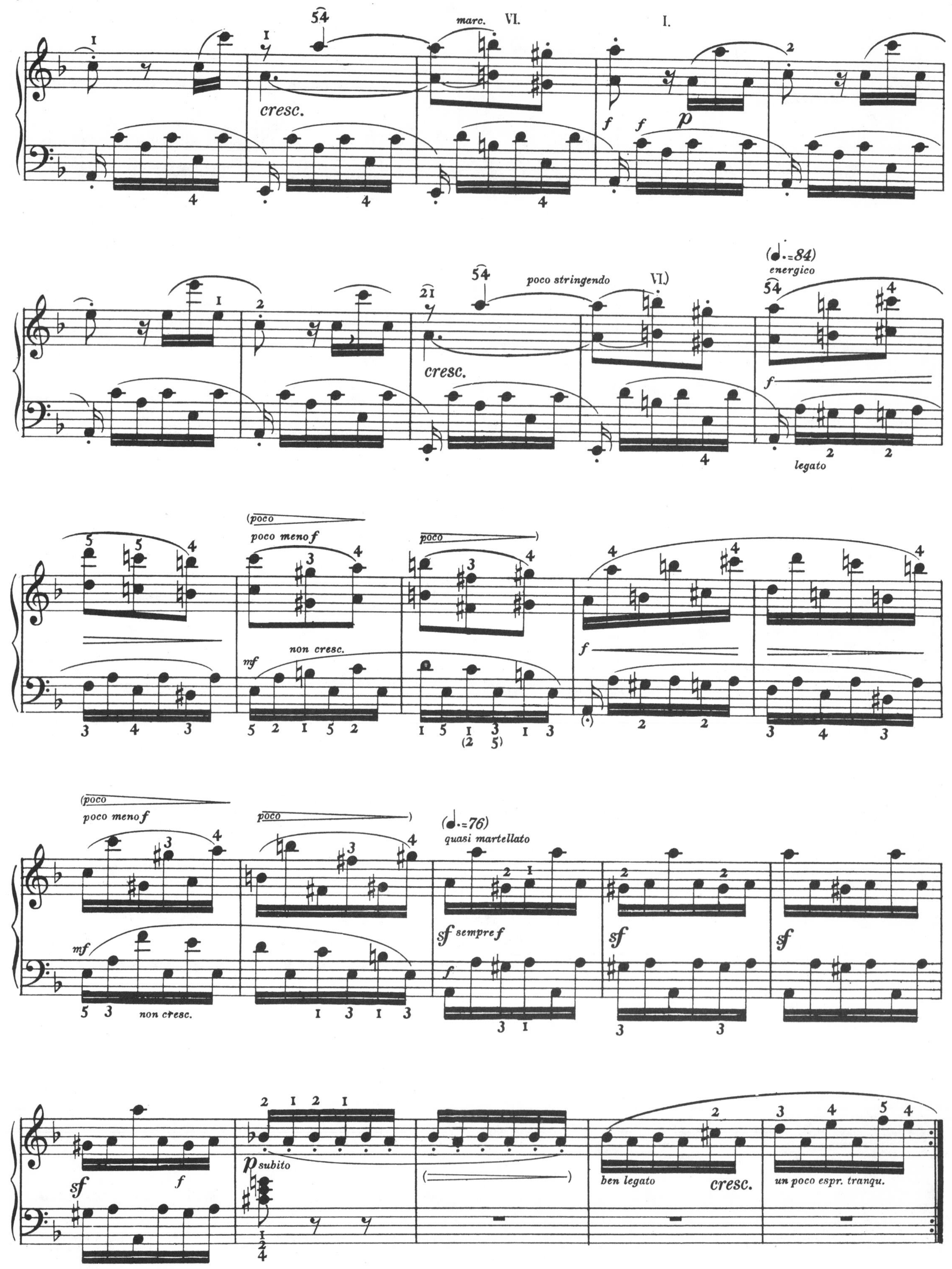
marc.
VI.
I.
cresc.
poco stringendo
VI.)
(♩.=84)
energico
cresc.
legato
(poco
poco meno f
non cresc.
poco
poco meno f
poco
(♩.=76)
quasi martellato
sf sempre f
non cresc.
p subito
ben legato
cresc.
un poco espr. tranqu.

i.t.
dolce
f subito
p subito
dolce
f
(♩.=84)
sempre f e marc.

(♩. = 92)
energico

a) Manche Ausgaben haben p erst zum vierten 16 tel; reizvoller (und vermutlich richtig) aber ist es, schon zweites und drittes 16 tel leise und recht ruhig zu spielen.

a) Dans plusieurs éditions le p n'est noté qu'à la quatrième double-croche; il est plus attrayant cependant (et probablement plus juste) de jouer piano et avec calme dès la deuxième et la troisième double-croche.

a) Some editions have p only at the fourth semiquaver; it is, however, more attractive (and, presumably, more correct) to play the foregoing second and third semiquavers softly and rather quietly, too.

sempre legato
cresc.
p
poco a poco
un poco stringendo
a)
sempre legato
a)
f
sempre f
sf
sempre un poco agitato, ma senza pressare
[p]
sempre p
a) Leichtere Ausführung:
Facilité:
Easier:
und zwei Takte weiter:
de même que deux mesures plus loin:
the same as the measures further on:

a) *Der Fingersatz ohne Klammern ist von Beethoven.*
Le doigté qui ne se trouve pas entre parenthèses est de Beethoven.
The unbracketed fingering is Beethoven's.

sf sempre f
sf
sf
sf
f
(♩.=84)
mf
non dim.
p
dim.
pp
poco a poco in tempo primo
(♩.=72)
p
semplice
poco
sempre legato
p
(♩.=76)
poco
p
cresc.

decresc.
p
cresc.
f
(♩.=84)
p subito
cresc.
f
p
cresc.
f
f
p
cresc.
f
f
ben marc.
non legato
sempre f
sf

a) v. p: 21 a)
f passionato
sempre non legato
Ped. *

232
v. p. 21 a)
non legato
sf
f
decresc.
p semplice
f
sf
dim.
mp
p
un poco stringendo
p
cresc.
sempre non legato
f
(♩. = 76) (I.
tranqu., ma in tempo
p subito
non legato
cresc.

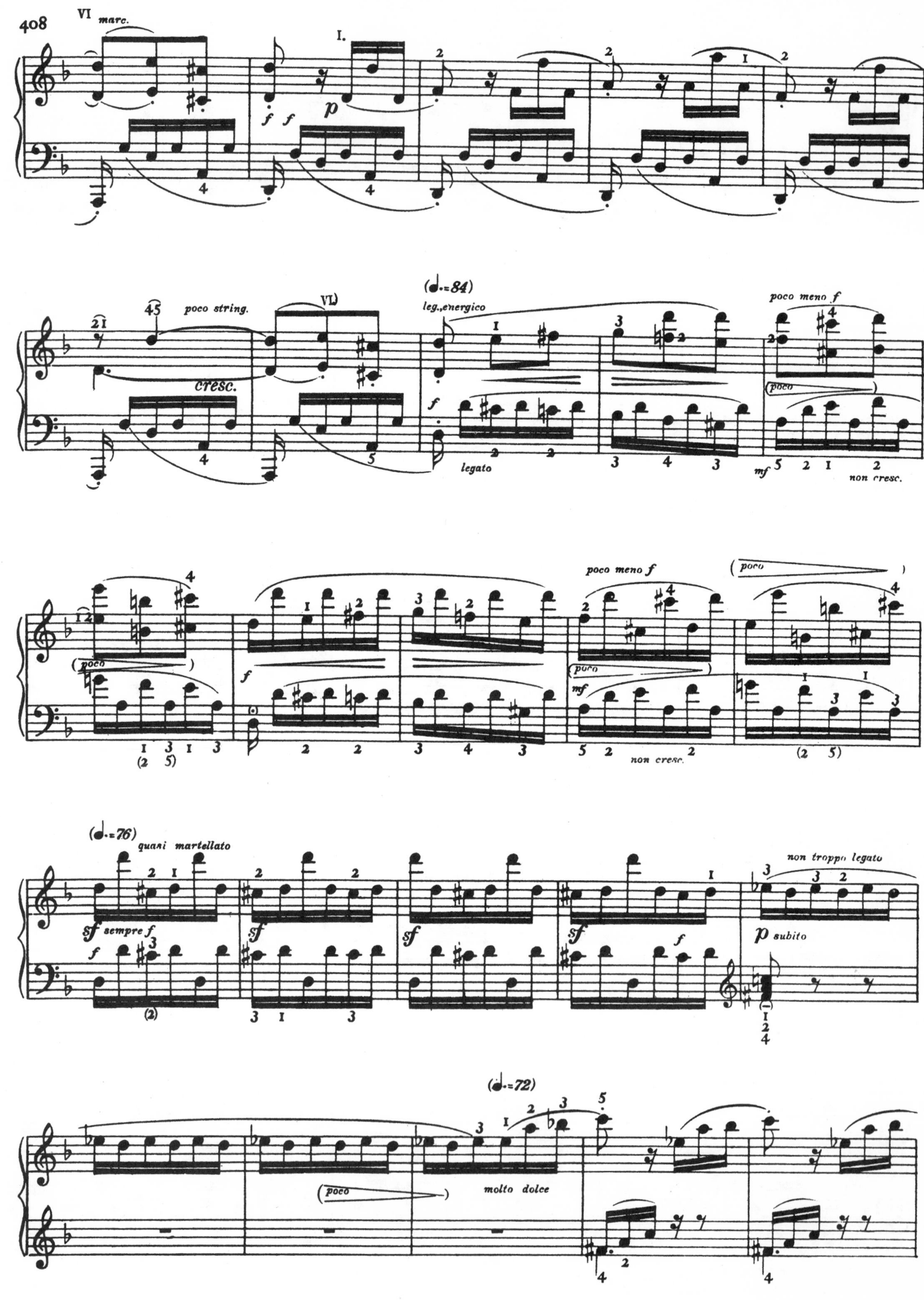
VI marc.
poco string.
cresc.
(♩.=84)
leg., energico
legato
poco meno f
poco
non cresc.
(♩.=76)
quasi martellato
sempre f
non troppo legato
p subito
(♩.=72)
molto dolce

cresc.
un poco espr.
dolce
semplice
dolce
cresc.
espr.
dim.
cresc.
dim.
molto

(♩. = 76)
pp
ff sempre
ten.
(tranqu.)
i. t.
ff
sempre legato
p
cresc.
dim.
Ped.
f
espr.

p
cresc.
f
sf più espr.
f
p
cresc.(più)
(I.
Ped.
(♩.=69)
ff
rubato, molto espr.
non dim.
VI)
tranquillo, molto semplice
ff
p dolce
sempre legato
più p
sempre ben tranqu.
cresc.
(♩.=63)
non stringere
f
p subito
semplice, tranqu.
pp